Spreadsheet Magic

SECOND EDITION

Includes CD-ROM with
Lesson Templates and Samples

Pamela Lewis

International Society for Technology in Education
EUGENE, OREGON • WASHINGTON, DC

Spreadsheet Magic SECOND EDITION

Pamela Lewis

Director of Publishing Jean Marie Hall	**Developmental Editor** Tracy Cozzens
Acquisitions Editor Scott Harter	**Copy Editor** Mary Snyder
Production Editor Lynda Gansel	**Book Design** Signe Landin and Kim McGovern
Production Coordinator Maddelyn High	**Cover Design** Signe Landin
Rights and Permissions Administrator Diane Durrett	**Layout and Production** Kim McGovern

International Society for Technology in Education (ISTE)

Washington, DC Office:
   1710 Rhode Island Ave., NW, Suite 900, Washington, DC 20036

Eugene, OR Office:
   175 West Broadway, Suite 300, Eugene, OR 97401-3003
Order Desk: 1.800.336.5191
Order Fax: 1.541.302.3778
Customer Service: orders@iste.org
Book Publishing: books@iste.org
Rights and Permissions: permissions@iste.org
Web site: www.iste.org

Second Edition
ISBN-10: 1-56484-224-X
ISBN-13: 978-1-56484-224-4

About ISTE

The International Society for Technology in Education (ISTE) is the premier membership organization for educators engaged in improving teaching and learning through the effective use of technology. ISTE is the trusted source for professional development, knowledge generation, advocacy, and leadership in education technology innovation.

ISTE Book Publishing works with experienced educators to develop and produce practical resources for classroom teachers, teacher educators, and technology leaders. Every manuscript we select for publication is carefully peer-reviewed and professionally edited. We look for content that emphasizes the effective use of technology where it can make a difference—increasing the productivity of teachers and administrators; helping students with unique learning styles, abilities, or backgrounds; collecting and using data for decision making at the school and district level; and creating dynamic, project-based learning environments that engage 21st century learners. We value your feedback on this book and other ISTE products. E-mail us at **books@iste.org**.

ISTE is home of the National Educational Technology Standards (NETS) Project, the National Educational Computing Conference (NECC), and the National Center for Preparing Tomorrow's Teachers to Use Technology (NCPT[3]). To find out more about these and other ISTE initiatives and to view our complete book list or request a print catalog, visit our Web site at **www.iste.org**. You'll find information about:

- ISTE, our mission, and our members
- Membership opportunities and services
- Online communities and special interest groups (SIGS)
- Professional development services
- Research & evaluation services
- Educator resources
- ISTE's National Technology Standards for Students, Teachers, and Administrators
- *Learning & Leading with Technology* magazine
- *Journal of Research on Technology in Education*

About the Author

Pam Lewis graduated from the University of Witwatersrand, with a B.A. degree in education. After teaching French, English, history, and mathematics, she completed a bachelor's degree in psychology at the University of South Africa. Lewis was appointed to the French subject committee in the province of Transvaal, designing curriculum and developing study guides for teachers. After immigrating to the United States, she worked as a part-time French teacher in Milwaukee, Wisconsin. During this time she completed an M.S. degree in computers in education at Cardinal Stritch University.

She currently works as a computer teacher/coordinator at a parochial school in southeastern Wisconsin, where she teaches computer classes to students in kindergarten through eighth grade and works with teachers to integrate technology in the curriculum. She also works part-time as a technology consultant, and has trained teachers in the Archdiocese of Milwaukee Schools and other school districts, doing some work for the Stephens Group. She has taught graduate classes for the Outreach Program of St. Mary's University of Minnesota, and for Cardinal Stritch University.

Acknowledgments

Thanks to the staff at St. Luke School—Kathy Adelmeyer, Chris Vogt, Jane Jonietz, Carole De Young, Nancy Grimm, Anne Hayes, Kathy Bowers, Julie Kadrich, Laurie Mertens, and Linda Osberg—for sharing their ideas and helping me improve the lessons. Thanks also to Principal Mary Laidlaw-Otto, and to the St. Luke parents for their support of the technology program at our school.

Thanks to Anita McAnear for helping with the first edition of this book, and to Scott Harter for his help with the second. I appreciate their insights, suggestions, and encouragement.

Contents

Introduction 1

Practical Magic **13**

How Spreadsheets Can Increase Teacher Productivity 14

Getting Started with Spreadsheets 19

■ A Complete Model Lesson—Creating Bingo Cards 22

Quick Reference Guide for Using Excel 29

Standards by Lesson 36

Scope and Sequence Chart of Spreadsheet Skills 38

Kindergarten Lessons **41**

1. Counting to 10 (MATH) 42

2. Classifying Nouns (LANGUAGE ARTS) 45

First-Grade Lessons **47**

3. Counting on a Grid (MATH) 48

■ Counting to 100 48

■ Counting by 2s, 3s, and 5s 51

■ Counting Large Numbers 53

4. March Weather Watch (MATH, SCIENCE, LANGUAGE ARTS) 55

■ March Calendar 55

■ Pictograph of March Weather 57

■ Bar Graph of March Weather 58

5. Recognizing Patterns (MATH) 60

6. Pets Survey (MATH) 64

Second-Grade Lessons **67**

7. Math Problems with 5, 7, and 9 (MATH) 68

■ Math Problems 1 68

■ Math Problems 2 70

8. Money to Spend (MATH) 72

9. Finding the Rule (MATH) 74

10. Change for a Bill (MATH) 77

   ■ Counting Up to Make Change 78

11. Apple-Tasting Survey (MATH) 80

12. Bats or Birds? (LANGUAGE ARTS, SCIENCE) 83

   ■ Comparisons 85

Third-Grade Lessons 87

13. Secret Message: Pledge of Allegiance (MATH, SOCIAL STUDIES) 88

14. Plot the Points on a Grid (MATH, SOCIAL STUDIES) 90

15. Creating a Multiplication Table (MATH) 93

16. Budgeting Money (MATH) 96

17. Counting Colored Candies (MATH) 99

18. Classifying Vertebrates (SCIENCE) 103

19. Brainstorming and Organizing Ideas (LANGUAGE ARTS) 105

   ■ Brainstorming from A to Z 106

   ■ Developing Ideas with Writing Prompts 107

   ■ Main Ideas and Details 108

   ■ Brainstorming on a Timeline 109

   ■ Making Comparisons on a Table 110

20. Designing Place Cards (MATH, LANGUAGE ARTS) 112

   ■ Compound Words 115

Fourth-Grade Lessons 117

21. Word Search (LANGUAGE ARTS) 118

22. Magic Square (MATH) 120

23. My Measurements (MATH) 123

24. Formulas for Converters (MATH, SCIENCE) 126

25. Visualizing Fractions (MATH) 128

   ■ Equivalent Fractions 129

   ■ Colored Fractions 130

   ■ Fractions: Greater Than or Less Than? 130

26. Music Survey (MATH, MUSIC) 134

27. States and Capitals (SOCIAL STUDIES) 138

Fifth-Grade Lessons 141

28. Science Dictionary (SCIENCE)..142

29. Decimals and Negatives (MATH)...144

- Decimals on a Grid 144
- Decimals on a Number Line...146
- Negative Numbers 147

30. **Finding Prime Numbers** (MATH)...149

31. **U.S. Weather Chart** (MATH, SCIENCE, SOCIAL STUDIES).................................152

32. **Concept Maps: Fairy Tales** (LANGUAGE ARTS)..155

33. **Planning a Road Trip** (LANGUAGE ARTS, SOCIAL STUDIES, MATH).................159

Sixth-Grade Lessons 161

34. Colored Candies: Ratio, Percentage, and Estimation (MATH)...........................162

35. Foreign Language Dictionary (LANGUAGE ARTS)...166

36. Using Formulas to Calculate Equations (MATH) 169

- Using Formulas to Make Basic Calculations..170
- Using Formulas to Evaluate Mathematical Expressions 172
- Using Formulas to Solve Mathematical Equations................................174

37. Travel Slideshow (MATH) 176

38. Analyzing Complex Patterns (MATH)..181

39. Probability with Coins and Dice (MATH)...184

40. Comparing Countries (SOCIAL STUDIES, MATH) 189

Appendix—National Educational Technology Standards
for Students (NETS•S)..191

Introduction

Welcome to the second edition of *Spreadsheet Magic*. The 40 lessons in this book provide step-by-step instructions for using spreadsheets to teach students in kindergarten through sixth grade. Spreadsheets were once thought of as a mathematics and accounting tool, but they have proven useful throughout the curriculum. The lessons that follow cover a variety of subject areas: language arts, social studies, science, music, and—of course—mathematics.

On the accompanying CD-ROM are the templates needed for each lesson, as well as samples showing how some of the lessons appear when completed. Extension Activities are also provided. The lessons are taught using Microsoft Excel, but the concepts can be applied to any spreadsheet program.

The Benefits of Spreadsheets

Why teach with spreadsheets? Spreadsheets are a powerful organizational tool for visual learners. They encourage higher-order thinking and help students develop, arrange, and connect ideas. Students benefit from the visual cues provided by the spreadsheet grid, the formatting of cell borders, various fills, and the use of clip art, formulas, charts, and numerical functions.

Working on computer rather than with pencil and paper helps motivate students to learn. Students love to play on computers and are motivated to complete tasks that might bore them using pen and paper. As I teach my students with spreadsheets, I find the computer engages them as they actively participate and create a product. They enjoy entering their spelling words into a spreadsheet, especially if they can use a tool to check the spelling and to sort words alphabetically.

Working on the computer also allows students to edit their work, correct errors, and print a professional-looking document. Colors and patterns are strong motivators, and students love to change font types and size and add borders of their own choosing. They also love to add clip art to their work.

But spreadsheets aren't just "fun" for students. Organizing data on a spreadsheet grid helps develop thinking skills such as sorting, categorizing, generalizing, comparing, and focusing on key elements. For instance, in the third-grade lesson Classification of Vertebrates, students use a spreadsheet to organize data they gather. As they conduct Internet research, students drag and drop data from Web sites to a spreadsheet, categorize the data in rows and columns, and then analyze and interpret the data.

In other lessons, students use the spreadsheet grid to organize words on a page to create products such as calendars; explore number patterns by counting by 7s; and solve a symmetry problem to create place cards. They sort words alphabetically to make a spelling list and a science dictionary. They match questions and answers to make their own flash cards, which helps them memorize math facts, foreign language vocabulary, or states and capitals.

In the Brainstorming and Organizing Ideas lesson, students begin with main ideas and develop details for writing a paragraph. In one part of the lesson, they are given prompts to expand as they explore the meaning of leadership, then relate their ideas to information they have learned about U.S. presidents (Figure I.1).

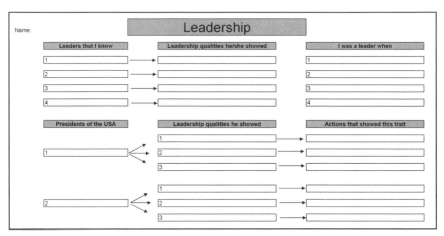

Figure I.1. When using the pre-formatted *Leadership* template, students only need to type in the spreadsheet cells, which will automatically expand as needed.

When using spreadsheets, very young students or students with learning disabilities don't have to rely on words they write. First-graders can use pictures to communicate ideas, such as in the first-grade lesson Classifying Nouns, where they drag clip art to one of three categories: person, place, or thing. In the fifth-grade Concept Maps: Fairy Tale lesson, students read a fairy tale online, analyze the story structure, and then use a concept map to outline their own version of the story.

By adapting the instructions in the third-grade Brainstorming on a Timeline lesson, teachers can create a variety of lessons. Social studies students can use a timeline to explore the sequence of actions in a famous person's life or in a period in history. Language arts students can use a timeline to construct a narrative. For instance, after brainstorming thoughts about significant firsts in their lives, students can then expand on one of the events by answering questions. They drag their answers into a logical order, and finally write a coherent paragraph (Figure I.2.).

	A	B	C	D	E	F	G	H	I	J	K	L
1	**Brainstorm Ideas on the Timeline**											
2	**The First Time I Proved My Strength, by Sammi**											
3												
4												
5	**Year:**	1997	1998	1999	2000	2001	2002	2003	2004	2005	2006	
6												
7	**My Age:**	1	2	3	4	5	6	7	8	9	10	
8								went on a				
9	**Event:**			moved to		first day	rode a	roller			broke a	
10				Springfield		of school	bike	coaster			board	
11												
12				**Choose one idea from above, and answer the questions below.**								
13	**Introduction: I'll never forget the first time I broke a board.**											
14												
15		3 months ago					Write answers here and drag them in order on the left.					
16		J.K. Lee karate dojo				*Who?*	Mom, Dad, and Tyler					
17		I broke a board with my hand.				*Why?*	Because it was my first time.					
18		My mom, dad, and Tyler were amazed.				*What?*	I broke a board with my hand.					
19						*When?*	3 months ago					
20						*Where?*	J.K. Lee karate dojo					
21	**Conclusion:**					*How?*	I felt proud.					
22		Because it was my first time, I felt proud.					My mom, dad, and Tyler were amazed					
23												

Figure I.2. The *Brainstorm Timeline* template is a good basis for prewriting activities.

Encouraging Higher-Order Thinking Skills

Using spreadsheets promotes higher-order thinking skills. Students engage in problem-solving and open-ended activities that have more than one "right" answer. As students complete the lessons in this book, they use the following higher-order thinking skills as defined in Bloom's Taxonomy: analysis, synthesis, and evaluation.

Analysis. In the first-grade Recognizing Patterns lesson, students analyze color and number patterns, then repeat them (Figure I.3). They analyze geography information in the Planning a Road Trip and Comparing Countries lessons. They classify animals as they categorize their characteristics in the second-grade lesson Bats or Birds? (Figure I.4).

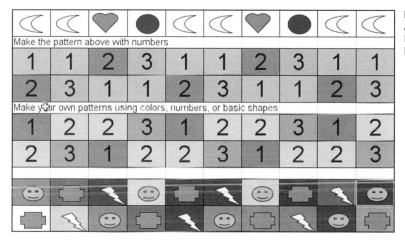

Figure I.3.
A completed Recognizing Patterns lesson.

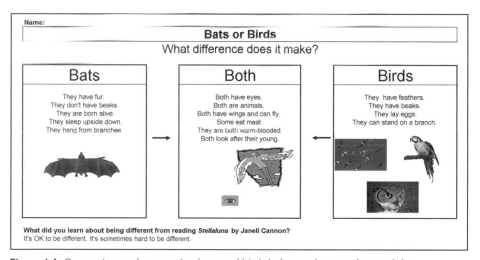

Figure I.4. Comparing and contrasting bats and birds helps students understand the characteristics of different kinds of animals.

Synthesis. Students synthesize information in numerous spreadsheet lessons. They make up their own patterns, math problems, and secret messages. They integrate and combine ideas, such as in the My Measurements and Travel Slideshow lessons. In the fourth-grade Music Survey lesson, they predict which type of music would be most popular with adults and children, organize their findings, and draw conclusions.

Evaluation. Students recognize subjectivity when they read the story of *Stellaluna* by Janell Cannon in the Bats or Birds? lesson. Discussing the story allows them to see the world from two different perspectives. Students make value judgments in lessons such as Apple-Tasting Survey, where they rank the flavor and texture of apples. When I teach this lesson, I find that my students sometimes struggle to rank their own favorite apple, having to make a hard choice between two that they like equally. In our class, we had a strict rule: only one choice for each ranking. Students needed prompting to decide on the class rankings after we counted the number of rankings of 1 for each apple. Figure I.5 shows a sample of the table they completed. Sorting their information correctly proved challenging for some students, but with help from the teacher and other students, they all successfully managed to fill out their tasting worksheet.

These are just a few examples of how students learn to use higher-order thinking skills while working with the spreadsheet lessons in this book.

Apples We Tasted		Name: Megan					
	Photo	Name of Apple	What It Looks Like	What It Tastes Like	My Ranking	Class Rankings of 1	Class Ranking
1		Gala	Reddish yellow	Very sweet	1	7	1
2		Red Delicious	Tall and dark red	It was dry, but sweet	6	4	3
3		Yellow Delicious	Yellowish green	Plain, not much flavor	5	0	6
4		Macintosh	It was half red and half green	Sour!	3	1	5
5		Jonathan	Dark red and round	Sour, but good	4	5	2
6		Granny Smith	Lime green	Tart and crisp	2	2	4

Figure I.5. Using spreadsheets, students completed an in-class survey of their taste in apples.

A Tool for Learning Mathematics

Beyond the benefits already mentioned, spreadsheets naturally offer benefits in teaching mathematics. The lessons in *Spreadsheet Magic* offer concrete ways to explore abstract concepts in mathematics, and offer special appeal to visual learners. Teaching math with spreadsheets gives students a stepping stone between the concrete use of manipulatives, such as blocks, and the abstract use of symbols to represent numbers. Mathematical ideas can be conveyed in several different ways (Figure I.6).

Exploring Colors, Borders, and Patterns

Students use color and pattern to shade areas of the spreadsheet grid, which helps them visualize addition and subtraction. The formatting of borders, font types, size, color, and pattern fill of cells helps focus student attention on key elements of a lesson, by visually organizing and highlighting data.

Spreadsheets: A Tool for Learning Mathematics

Visual Tool		Algebraic Functions, Use of Formulas	
Format borders Fill cells with color or pattern Insert clip art	Patterns Number sense Visualize abstract concepts Recognize symmetry Spatial reasoning	Use a ready-made formula Make up a formula Fill a formula right or down Change a variable and see the effect	Formulate, generalize Convert measurements Solve problems Develop, evaluate mathematical arguments

Organizational Tool		Computer Generated Charting	Numerical Functions
Use the grid Resize cells Format borders, fill Sort alphabetically Sort numerically	Patterns Number sense Coordinate geometry Number lines Multiplication tables Charts Calendars Timelines Magic squares	Make graphs Organize, represent, interpret data Communicate data	Make calculations Generate random numbers Format numbers • Fractions • Decimals • Currency

Figure I.6. This chart provides an overview of the numerous ways spreadsheets can enhance the curriculum.

Creating a Number Line

Students use the grid as a number line in several lessons. In the second-grade lesson Math Problems, students fill cells with color, allowing them to see how the colored cells relate to numbers on a number line (Figure I.7). In the fifth-grade lesson Decimals and Negatives, students learn more complex math concepts as they arrange numbers in ascending order on a number line (Figure I.8).

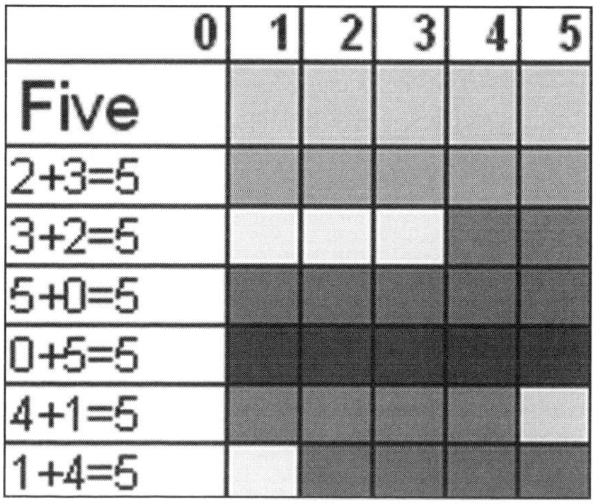

Figure I.7. Students fill cells with color to equal equations in the Math Problems lesson.

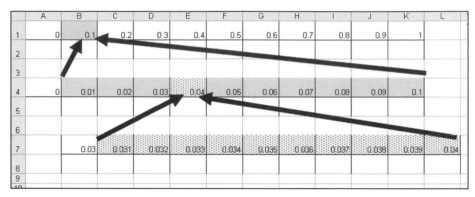

Figure I.8. The *Decimals Demo* template is a good place to start the Decimals on a Line lesson.

Exploring Patterns

The grid of cells encourages the exploration of patterns using color, numbers, and formulas to make rules. In the lesson Counting to 100, first-graders examine patterns on a partially filled-in 100s chart. They notice that the numbers are arranged in patterns when they count by 10s. They quickly see the number in the 1s place is the same for all numbers in a column—2, 12, 22, 32, 42, and so on—and they often choose to fill in the numbers going down rather than across. They become aware of their own mistakes as they notice, for example, that they get to a number ending in 0 before the end of the row (Figure I.9).

Figure I.9.
Spreadsheets help students see number patterns.

1	2	3	4	5	6	7	8	9	10
11	12	13	14	15	16	17	18	19	20
21	22	23	24	25	26	27	28	29	30
31	32	33	34	35	36	37	38	39	40
41	42	43	44	45	46	47	48	49	50
51	52	53	54	55	56	57	58	59	60
61	62	63	64	65	66	67	68	69	70
71	72	73	74	75	76	77	78	79	80
81	82	83	84	85	86	87	88	89	90
91	92	93	94	95	96	97	98	99	100

Count by 2s	(Fill with red)
Count by 5s	(Underline)
Count by 3s	(Fill with pattern)

Patterns become more complex as students get older. In Complex Patterns, sixth-graders explore patterns where numbers change by a rule, and they complete patterns like the Fibonacci pattern, where a more complex rule changes the numbers. They also use equations to describe patterns. (See Using and Generating Formulas.)

Plotting Coordinates

With the Creating Bingo Cards lesson, students learn to identify a cell name and its location, such as B1, N3, G4. Third-graders locate points on a grid in Secret Message: Pledge of Allegiance, and again in Plot Points on a Grid, where they plot given coordinates to create an outline of the United States.

Making Charts

Charts add meaning to information, helping students analyze and interpret data. In *Spreadsheet Magic*, students make charts from spreadsheet records, learning to organize their ideas and present information to an audience. The Excel program can easily generate bar, line, and pie charts from data.

Pie charts reinforce the idea of percentages as a portion of a whole. Students use pie charts to compare ratios in Colored Candies: Ratio, Percentage, and Estimation. In March Weather Watch (Figure I.10), students make their own bar graphs by filling cells with color as they interpret weather data. They add clip art to bar graphs in the pictograph portion of the lesson.

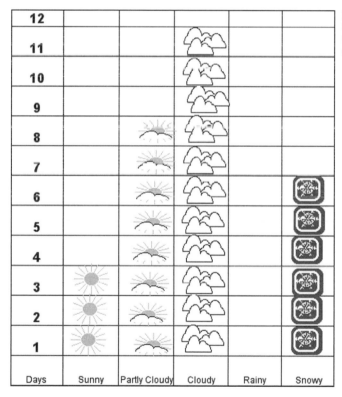

Figure I.10.
Students fill cells with clip art to create pictographs.

Second-graders chart the results of an Apple-Tasting Survey. In Count the Colored Candies, third-graders graph the percentage of various colored candies in a single bag, and for all students in class. Fourth-graders compare personal measurements at the beginning and end of the school year in My Measurements, and they use charts to evaluate the results of the Music Survey.

Throughout the program, students will gradually become confident in their ability to generate and interpret charts. By fourth grade, they can format a chart, changing the title, scale, and smallest and largest values on the Y-axis, and show gridlines and data labels.

Using and Generating Formulas

Templates for many of the lessons are built with formulas, so that students focus on problem solving while the computer makes the calculations for them. These lessons include Change for a Bill, Money to Spend, and Magic Square.

In other lessons, students create their own formulas, allowing them to explore how and why formulas are used, and how changing a variable affects the outcome. Students use formulas to multiply in the Multiplication Table lesson; in the Formulas for Converters lesson, students make up various formulas to create a calculator.

In other lessons, students use formulas to generalize a rule (Find the Rule), to make conversions (Formulas for Converters and Travel Slideshow), to calculate budget totals (Travel Slideshow), and to calculate ratios (Colored Candies: Ratio, Percentage, and Estimation). They make predictions, asking "What if . . ."-type questions, as they change a value and investigate the effect on numbers in other cells. Soon, students discover how they can generalize formulas using the Fill Down and Fill Right functions. They feel the power of spreadsheets as they extend formulas to additional cells with the click of a mouse. They see how a formula can make the computer simulate flipping coins and tossing dice.

Scaffolding Technology Skills and Concepts

The lessons in *Spreadsheet Magic* provide scaffolding of computer skills. Learning of these skills is structured so that young students don't need to know how to use all the tools in this powerful program. They begin by opening the templates provided on the enclosed CD-ROM. On these templates, much of the formatting has been done for them. Students then modify the file as they complete the lesson, and save it in their own folders or a designated space on the computer or network.

As they progress through *Spreadsheet Magic*, students will gradually develop the spreadsheet skills listed below. Each lesson identifies the specific spreadsheet skills students will practice in that lesson. Although these skills are gradually mastered through the use of spreadsheets, they are helpful in a variety of computer applications, including Microsoft Word and PowerPoint. For a detailed list of the skills students will master, see the Scope and Sequence Chart of Spreadsheet Skills.

- Enter and format text and numbers in cells

- Fill cells with color and patterns

- Insert clip art from the Excel Clip Gallery

- Resize and move pictures

- Duplicate graphics and place them in cells

- Resize rows or columns

- Sort data in alphabetical and numerical order

- Create graphs and charts

- Move and resize charts

- Navigate around the spreadsheet using the arrows, Tab, Enter, Home, End, Ctrl Home, and Ctrl End keys

- Use ready-made formulas

- Insert and delete cells, rows, and columns

- Use Drag & Drop to move, cut, and paste cell contents

- Use Ctrl Drag & Drop to copy and paste cell contents

- Access clip art from Microsoft Office Online's Clip Art and Media Web page; download and insert pictures into Excel documents

- Format cell borders

- Use Drawing toolbar including text boxes, lines, arrows.

- Format charts

- Insert text boxes, use arrows or lines

- Make up original formulas

- Generalize formulas by filling right or down

- Format alignment and text wrap

- Format numbers as currency, decimals, fractions, and percentages

- Use Print Preview and Page Setup

- Show toolbars, add and remove toolbar icons

- Insert hyperlinks

- Set print options (show grid; show column and row headings)

Student Motivation in a Risk-Free Environment

Students love to play on computers and are motivated to complete tasks that might bore them using pen and paper. They are engaged as they actively participate and create a product. They enjoy entering their spelling words into a spreadsheet, especially if they can use a tool to check the spelling and to sort words alphabetically. Color and pattern are strong motivators, and students love to change font types and size and add borders of their own. They also love to add clip art to personalize their work.

Working on computers in a risk-free and dynamic environment encourages students to be more adventurous. They find it easy to correct errors, make changes, and improve on their ideas. Students take pride in the pleasing presentation of the work they create: lines are straight, writing is clear, and pictures are perfect for *all* students, not only the best natural artists. Using templates or digital worksheets structures an activity and guides student learning. The templates in *Spreadsheet Magic* have been saved with instructions, prompts, and specific formatting that improves presentation and speeds up completion of the task. Students as young as kindergartners begin learning with technology as they work in spreadsheets knowing only a few spreadsheet skills.

Practical Tips for Using Spreadsheet Magic

As a computer lab teacher, I work with classroom teachers to select lessons related to what students are studying. Each computer lesson is introduced when the class is learning about that particular theme or concept. Often, as part of their preparation, students complete a written lesson before they arrive at the lab. After students work on the computers, I typically provide a follow-up activity. The lessons in this book were easily completed by students and were considered to be effective learning tools by the teachers.

In the computer lab, I have students work alone or in a small group at a computer station. The lessons may also be used in a one-computer classroom with a projection device as a class activity, or without a projection device with small groups taking turns using the computer. Students who have completed the lesson can show the next group of students how to do the lesson.

I recommend that the teacher demonstrate the lesson before the students begin, either on a computer attached to a projector or by having students gather around a single computer. However, the students will create, develop, and design as they work on each new spreadsheet lesson. They will make their own decisions about where to begin and how to proceed as they solve the problem of how to create the end product. When each student masters a task, he or she can become a helper, teaching other students how to do the work.

I do not generally give lengthy written instructions to students. Most students in the elementary and primary grades find it hard to follow written instructions, yet they are able to learn the computer skills necessary for the lessons. In place of written instructions, they watch a live demonstration of the project. I write out keywords and instructions on a white board, such as the name of a menu, a word to select from a menu, or what to name a file.

Where written student instructions are part of the lesson, such as Plot the Points on a Grid and Prime Numbers, these instructions should be copied and handed out to students.

Most of these lessons can be completed in a single 45-minute period, but allowing 10 minutes to set up between classes is a good idea. Use this time to open the program and the template before students arrive at the lab or classroom. If teaching consecutive classes, this extra 10 minutes allows slow workers time to complete and print their lesson after class ends.

Every student needs to have a copy of the template from the enclosed CD-ROM at his or her computer station or laptop. Templates are generally not as detailed for older students, who do more of the formatting themselves, but they may include more instructions. Samples of some of the more complex lessons involving formulas are also on the CD-ROM.

Please note: The teacher who purchases this book is licensed to make copies of the templates for use with her or his own classes. Each teacher who uses the lessons needs to purchase a separate copy of the book.

What You Need to Teach from Spreadsheet Magic

Spreadsheet Magic instructions are written for use with **Microsoft Excel**, but the lessons could easily be done with a different spreadsheet program, such as Apple-Works or Microsoft Works.

The lessons are arranged by grade level, from kindergarten through sixth grade. Each lesson includes a description of the lesson, the spreadsheet skills that will be practiced, the national standards addressed, the steps on the computer, and extension lessons designed to challenge students who finish the main lesson quickly. Some activities, such as Spelling List 1 or Beginning Letters Bingo, can be used for multiple grade levels.

Internet access is required for the completion of some of the lessons. If teachers do not have access to the Internet, they can provide alternate sources of information, such as books or clip art on CD-ROM. Microsoft Office Online's Clip Art and Media Web page is an excellent resource for thousands of clip art pictures and photographs.

The enclosed CD-ROM provides all of the Excel templates used in the lessons. Teachers are encouraged to change the templates in this book to meet their students' needs, and to modify the existing lessons for remediation or extension. For example, patterns that first-graders find too difficult to complete may be changed to suit the individual right at their workstation. Teachers can lock cells to protect information that students shouldn't be able to delete, or hide cells so that answers that autoscore a worksheet aren't visible. On some templates, formulas are inserted to automatically check and tally answers.

A projector that attaches to a computer is useful for demonstrating skills. Alternatively, students can gather around one computer screen to see the demonstration. Data projectors are easy to hook up to a computer, and they project onto a screen or onto a wall.

A color printer is strongly recommended for many of the lessons in this book. It seems strange to me that teachers who encourage elementary students to use crayons and paints are often reluctant to use color printing. Color adds to the visual effect and is a strong motivator for students. If used sparingly, the color printer does not add a large amount to costs, although it is necessary to buy color print cartridges, and the cost per page for printing color is higher than for black and white. We use a Hewlett-Packard color laser printer very successfully in our lab.

A computer network can be useful for file management. Our lab of 30 networked computers allows students to open the templates on a shared folder, where they have read-only privileges. Working on a shared document facilitates collaboration.

Students in kindergarten and first grade save the document with the help of an adult, while students in second grade and up save their work in their own folders on the server. The documents may be deleted after the lessons are completed and printed. If computers aren't networked, the files can be opened from the CD-ROM, renamed, and saved to the hard drive.

Instructional Support

For most lessons in grades 1 through 3, the classroom teacher is involved and present in the lab, as well as myself, and classes often have additional help from a parent volunteer. Students need to have their work checked before they print it, by an adult or a student who has successfully completed the task and been assigned as a helper. They should only print their work after they have corrected all of their mistakes.

As with other areas of schoolwork, there is a vast range of student ability to success-fully complete a task on a computer within a given time. Students are encouraged to help each other as they complete the lessons. For many lessons, I have provided extension lessons to use with students who work fast, allowing slower students more time to complete their work. Students should be encouraged to always save their work before they print it to avoid losing it if unforeseen problems occur.

Assessment

I recommend that the teacher check their students' progress and provide immediate feedback. Completion of a *Spreadsheet Magic* lesson often demonstrates that students understand concepts previously introduced in the classroom. The lessons address the National Educational Technology Standards for Students (NETS•S), as well as subject-area standards, as indicated in each lesson. See the appendix for NETS•S.

New to This Edition

In choosing the content for this second edition of *Spreadsheet Magic*, every lesson from the first edition was stringently reviewed. Several lessons have been replaced with entirely new lessons that better illustrate the broad application of spreadsheets in today's classroom. The previous format—offering dual instructions for Excel and AppleWorks—has been revised to include only Excel instructions to improve the accessibility of the lessons. Remember: any of these lessons can be taught with your choice of spreadsheet program. A Teacher Productivity section has been added, replacing previous appendixes on basic program use that offered less specific infor-mation for today's working teacher. Finally, the entire book has been redesigned to improve its usability in your classroom.

Enjoy the magic of spreadsheets with your students!

Reference

Bloom, B.S. (1956). *Taxonomy of Educational Objectives, Handbook 1: The Cognitive Domain*. New York: David McKay.

Practical Magic

How Spreadsheets Can Increase Teacher Productivity

Getting Started with Spreadsheets

Quick Reference Guide for Using Excel

Standards by Lesson

Scope and Sequence Chart of Spreadsheet Skills

How Spreadsheets Can Increase Teacher Productivity

As teachers, the templates and instructions for *Spreadsheet Magic* lessons don't require us to be experts in using spreadsheet programs. We're focusing on the educational purpose for incorporating spreadsheets in the classroom.

However, more and more, educators are required to make data-driven decisions. Spreadsheets are a great help in collecting and organizing that data. Once organized, we can use spreadsheets to create tables and charts that communicate our findings.

As you become more proficient in using spreadsheet programs, you will find even more uses for spreadsheets, such as creating checklists, seating charts, curriculum guides, and even lesson plans. A powerful spreadsheet program such as Excel can increase your productivity in numerous ways. You can use it to

- Alphabetize lists of names, or rank scores according to grades by sorting data.

- Make class lists, checklists and rubrics, and even seating charts, by using the grid.

- Count students with failing grades, A grades, or work not turned in with Excel's automatic functions.

- Include in your digital lesson plans links to Web pages, standards, samples of student work, and templates.

- Create interactive drill-and-practice digital worksheets that give students immediate feedback and eliminate the need to correct them by hand. For details about personalizing the worksheets provided on the CD-ROM, see Getting Started with Spreadsheets.

Figure TP.1 shows which skills are necessary for which educational and productivity tasks.

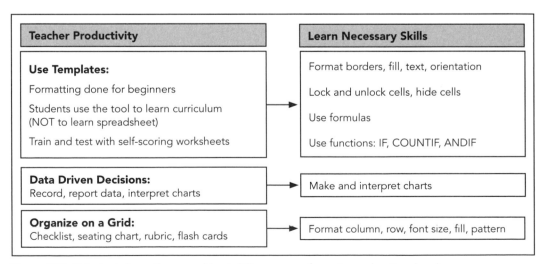

Figure TP.1. This chart shows the spreadsheet skills necessary for various educational and productivity tasks.

Alphabetize Class Lists

Storing class rosters in spreadsheets is a time-saver. To create a class list, enter student names in a column in random order. You can instantly sort them into alphabetical order by highlighting the names, clicking on the Data menu, then choosing Sort in ascending order. Once you have entered the names, you may want to enter headings for columns to the right of the names. To change the angle of text in the heading row (which can save space), highlight the cells you want to change, click on the Format menu, and then on Cells (Figure TP.2). Click on the Alignment tab and change the Orientation.

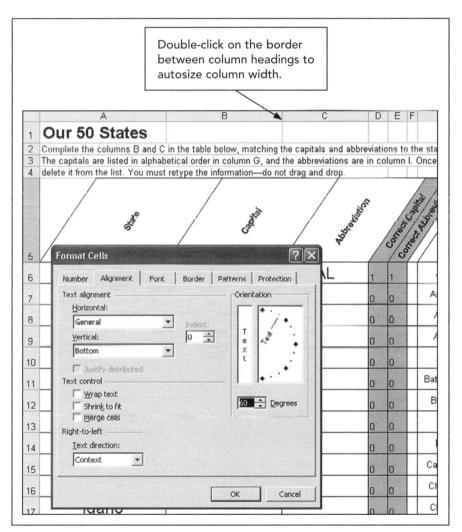

Figure TP.2. You can easily angle text in a spreadsheet.

Grading sheets, rubrics, or checklists can be made using the grid format. These can be printed out for students to use (Figure TP.3). They may also be scored on computer and some criteria may be given a heavier weighting. The formula for calculating the total would reflect this.

Readers's Name:		Enter 3 for excellent, 2 for satisfactory, 1 for needs improvement					
Story Scoring Chart	**Story Number**						
Title	Relates to story, catchy						
Characters	We get t know and care about the characters, we learn what they are like by their actions						
Setting	Imaginative, detailed, helps bring the story to life						
Tone/Voice	Is appropriate for young children						
Personality/ Originality	Interesting, individual, original and unique, has well-developed personality						
Language	Simple language used well, creates picutes in your mind, easy to read aloud, we understand what the author means						
Mechanics	Sounds like it has been proofread, no big errors						
Introduction	A strong beginning gets the reader's attention, you want to read further						
Organization/ Plot	Story is easy to follow, there is a problem that is solved. It has a high point and a clear ending						
Illustrations	Adds meaning, high quality, has particular style						
Total Score							
%							
Ranking							

Figure TP.3. Students review each other's picture stories with this spreadsheet.

It's often helpful to include instructions on the spreadsheet, as in Figure TP.4.

Name:
Checklist for Introduction to HTML

Appropriate title	<TITLE > ... </ TITLE>
Centered text	<CENTER > ... </CENTER>
Left aligned text	<LEFT> ... </LEFT>
Line breaks	
New Paragraphs	<P>
Bolded text	<B> ... </B>
Italicized text	<I> ... </I>
Scrolling text	<MARQUEE> ... </MARQUEE>
Image inserted (Saved in same folder as the Web page, in jpg format)	<IMG SRC="...JPG>
Name a bookmark on your page	<A NAME="...">
Link to a place on your page	<A HREF="#.."> Describe the link</A>
Link to a different Web page address	link</A>
Format background color	<BODYBGCOLOR="#$$$$$$>
Format text colors	<BODYTEXT="#$$$$$$>
Format link colors	<BODYLINK="#$$$$$$>
Format visited links	<BODYVLINK="#$$$$$$>
Visually appealing	Colors, graphics
Clear, easy to read	Fonts, line breaks, alignment
Includes information about the author of this page	Who you are, why you are writing this
Includes acknowledgement of source of information	Used Citation machine to generate reference http://citationmachine.net/

Figure TP.4. A checklist for students inputting HTML code to format a Web page.

Create a Seating Chart

To create a seating chart that maps your classroom (Figure TP.5), start with a blank spreadsheet. Format borders around cells to show that a desk is positioned there. Enter student names in those cells. Change the column width by highlighting a column and holding down the Ctrl key to highlight cells that aren't adjacent. Click on the Format menu, on Column, then Column Width, and enter an appropriate size.

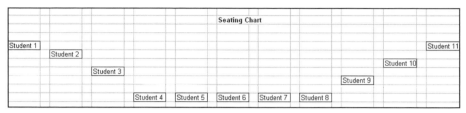

Figure TP.5. A teacher can create a handy seating chart using a spreadsheet.

Create Useful Classroom Management Documents

Teachers who are proficient users of Excel will enjoy using the program to create lesson plans, curriculum guides, or records of work completed by students. Teachers can easily save and access information. They can sort it by date or by a type of information, such as state standards. Spreadsheets are easily updated, and can be linked to related files.

Spreadsheets can include comments and details that will pop up only when you move your mouse over a cell. To create a comment, right-click the target cell and left-click on Insert Comment.

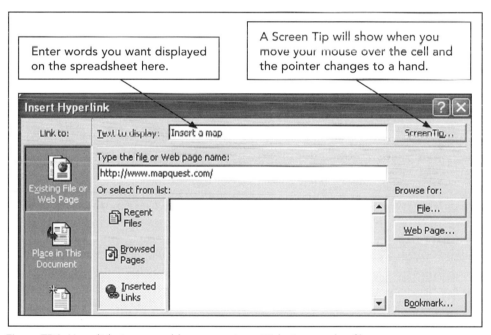

Figure TP.6. Hyperlinks in a spreadsheet can point to Web sites or other files.

You can further annotate your spreadsheets by inserting hyperlinks. Hyperlinks can point to files such as templates and samples of student work, either created in Excel or in other programs. After a hyperlink has been inserted, the mouse pointer will change to a hand shape when you move it over the cell containing the hyperlink. If you click on the cell, the designated document or Web site will open. To do this, right-click the target cell, and left-click on Hyperlink, and the window shown in Figure TP.6 will open up.

Use Excel's Automatic Functions

You don't have to type in every date you want on your spreadsheet. You can fill dates or pick from a list of words already entered to avoid tedious typing. For instance, enter a date in a cell, then enter a second date under it, such as one week later, or one fortnight later, or one month later. You can then highlight the two cells and Fill Down by dragging on the right bottom corner. Excel figures out that you're creating a sequence, and will enter the rest of the dates for you (Figure TP.7).

You can also insert repeated text without retyping it. Right-click a cell and click on Pick from List to insert text that has been put in a cell above. This saves time typing in a list of names, repeated student comments, or state standards. Just open the pop-up list, click on your selection, and the text is inserted into the cell (Figure TP.8).

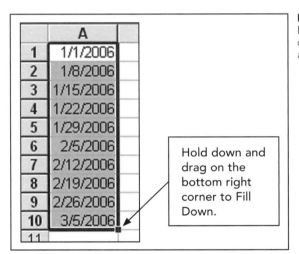

Hold down and drag on the bottom right corner to Fill Down.

Figure TP.7.
Enter just two dates to create a sequence.

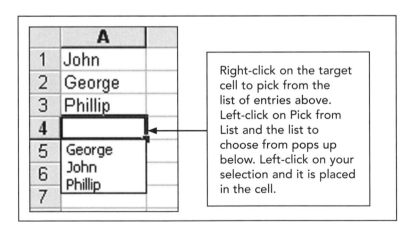

Right-click on the target cell to pick from the list of entries above. Left-click on Pick from List and the list to choose from pops up below. Left-click on your selection and it is placed in the cell.

Figure TP.8.
Pick from entries you have created to avoid tedious typing.

Have Fun!

Try using spreadsheets in your classroom for more than just lessons. You may find, as I have, that new uses and opportunities occur to you as you learn more about their capabilities. Explore everything you can do with spreadsheets. Don't be afraid to experiment. Not only will you find that your productivity increases, you'll have fun along the way.

Getting Started with Spreadsheets

This chapter will help you get started with spreadsheets in the classroom, whether you are a long-time Excel user or a spreadsheet "newbie." It introduces three basic spreadsheet activities—word lists, flash cards, and bingo cards—and demonstrates how you can modify the lessons in this book to fit the skill level(s) and age group(s) you are teaching. If you are new to spreadsheets, try one of these basic activities first, pulling up the appropriate template on the accompanying CD-ROM and filling it in with the words or math problems or science facts that your students are currently learning. Don't be afraid to experiment—modify the worksheet to better fit the needs of your classroom. If problems arise that you can't fix, simply close the worksheet without saving it, reopen the template on the CD-ROM and start over again.

The Power of Personalized Worksheets

This book provides teachers with templates that they can modify for students to use. Working in an easy-to-change, digital format is very different than using a hard copy. Lessons can be tailored to the needs of specific students, or to the particular needs of a class, if a teacher modifies how students will use them. All the teacher needs to do is change the template provided with a lesson in this book, then save his or her own version of the lesson. That will become the template that students open to begin the assignment.

Three examples of lessons that could apply to different subject areas and grade levels have been included in this section to demonstrate the potential for personalizing these lessons. This principle may be applied to most of the lessons in this book. Because of this adaptability, teachers are encouraged to look at all of the lessons in this book, not just the ones for their grade level.

Word Lists

Younger students can use spreadsheets to check spelling and categorize words. For instance, they can enter a list of spelling words in column A, sort them in alphabetical order, and insert pictures to illustrate them. In column B, they can write a sentence using the word, or write a definition of the word. If you make a template for such an exercise, you will need to widen columns, wrap text, widen rows, format borders, and instruct the students on how to sort alphabetically. The fifth-grade Science Dictionary lesson provides detailed instructions on making such a list.

You may also give students a list of words and jumbled definitions, and ask them to match the words with the correct definitions. Start by entering the words and definitions in correct order. Then sort the definitions column in alphabetical order to mix them up. To do this, highlight the list of definitions, click on the Data menu, then choose Sort. Insert a column between the words and the list of definitions to give students room to work. Simply highlight the column containing definitions, click on the Insert menu, and on Column. Students will work such a lesson by dragging the contents of the definition cells to match the correct words.

Flash Cards

Flash cards are useful for drill and practice of mathematics, social studies, or science facts. When students create their own flash cards for future review, you want to make sure they don't learn from work that has errors. Create worksheets for students that give them immediate feedback. Have students enter their answers, and as they do so, the computer can check the accuracy of math facts or spelling. The formulas inserted in the flash cards template will check for the answer that you determine is the correct one. You can use the templates provided on the CD-ROM and not bother with formulas. If you decide you would like to generate your own worksheets, some understanding of how spreadsheet formulas work will be helpful. The templates for *Flash Cards*, *Flash Cards-3 Columns*, and *States Flash Cards* are ready for student use.

You don't need to understand how these self-scoring worksheets work to use them. Simply open the template called *Flash Cards-3 Columns* and enter the answers you want the computer to score in the feedback column, where it says Great Job! or Try Again.

F26	▼		=	=COUNTIF(F6:F25,"=Great		
A	B	C		D	E	F
Prepared for 5th grade students by Megan J. and Jo						
Order of Operations						
Name:						
BODMAS	( )	Of / * + -				
	1	4-9/3+5		=	6	Great Job
	2	(3*7)+(64/8)		=		Try again
	3	20+6/3-7		=		Try again
	4	18*(11-6)		=		Try again
	5	2+(3*6)+10		=		Try again
	6	(28+32)*4		=		Try again
	7	8*2/2+24		=		Try again
	8	3+5*10/2+8		=		Try again
	9	59-45/5*3+41		=		Try again
	10	10*4+(49/7)*2		=		Try again
	11	18-3/3+(63/3)-6		=		Try again
	12	(28/7)+5-3+(7*2)		=		Try again
	13	(4*8)-5+(6-6)		=		Try again
	14	16/4+2*6		=		Try again

Figure GS.1. The COUNTIF function can total numbers in cells and display an encouraging phrase.

If you want to understand how these formulas work so that you can modify them for additional worksheets, then read further.

The formula to check the answer in a cell is as follows: =IF(B1=7, "Great Job!","Try Again."). You enter what you would like it to say in quotation marks if the answer in cell B1 is correct and if it is incorrect. This basically says that if the answer in B1 is 7, then the words "Great Job!" will appear. If anything other than 7 is entered, the words "Try Again." will appear. This function can be used for checking numerical answers, as in multiplication table flash cards.

Excel spreadsheets can also total the number of correct answers using the COUNTIF function. Figure GS.1 shows an example an Order of Operations exercise made by seventh graders for a fifth-grade class. Excel totals the number of correct responses. In the formula the students used, =COUNTIF(F6:F25, "Great Job!"), the range F6: F25 indicates the cells the computer should check for the correct total.

The spreadsheet can also be used to check words that students enter, but they must be spelled exactly as they are in the formula. For an example of this, see the fourth-grade lesson States and Capitals.

Protect Your Spreadsheets

When students use a template from the book, or when you create your own template, you may want to lock certain cells so that important information can't be deleted or changed. Row and column height and width will also be locked. By default all cells are locked, so you need to unlock the cells where you want students to make changes before you protect the worksheet. It is important to unlock specific cells, or you will lock all the cells in the spreadsheet when you protect the sheet. Highlight the cells you want to remain unlocked, click on the Format menu, and on Cells and on the Protection tab. Remove the check mark next to Locked (Figure GS.2). Next, turn on protection, click on the Tools menu, and on Protection, and on Protect Sheet. You can set a password for unlocking this protection if you wish.

You can move between unlocked cells on a protected worksheet by clicking on an unlocked cell, and then pressing the Tab key on the keyboard. If cells are locked on a template and you wish to modify that template, simply click on the Tools menu, click on Protection, and choose Unprotect sheet.

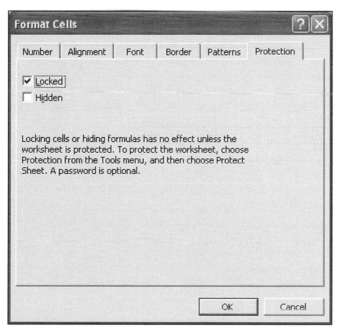

Figure GS.2.
Unlock cells you want students to change, then protect the spreadsheet.

A Complete Model Lesson—Creating Bingo Cards

Students love to play bingo. Bingo is a good way to review letters, vocabulary, or math facts and is easily adaptable for any grade level. The following lesson also introduces the structural format for all of the lessons in this book:

- **Description** of the lesson, exercise or activity

- **Higher-Order Thinking Skills** used in the lesson

- **Spreadsheet Skills Practiced** in the lesson

- **Subject Areas and Standards Addressed** in the lesson

- **Computer Activity**—step-by-step instructions for completing the lesson

- **Extension** activities for expanding the lesson or adapting it to different skill levels

I. Creating Bingo Cards

Lesson Description

In this lesson, students make bingo boards for a variety of uses. In Beginning Letters Bingo, the board is used to review alphabet letters. In Math Facts Review Bingo, students solve simple problems in addition, subtraction, multiplication, or division. The bingo game students play after they have made their boards is a great incentive for them in working on this lesson.

Higher-Order Thinking Skills	Spreadsheet Skills Practiced	Subject Areas and Standards Addressed
Identify beginning letters	Enter text in a cell	NETS•S: 1, 3
Apply knowledge of beginning letters to match them with pictures	Select a picture	English Language Arts: 3
	Move a picture	Mathematics: 1, 3
Create a bingo card with math problems	Print a document	

Beginning Letters Bingo

Exercise Description

Students make their own bingo cards to review letters of the alphabet. They accomplish this by placing a picture and the beginning letter for that picture in a spreadsheet cell. When all students have completed the lesson, the class plays bingo using the boards they created on the computer. Students enjoy playing the game, and they master reading skills as they make the bingo card, then play the game.

Computer Activity

1. Students open the *Beginning Letters Bingo* template and type in their names.

2. The *Beginning Letters Bingo* template uses the letters a, b, c, e, f, g, h, m, p, r, s, t, w, and y. The teacher may want to identify the pictures at the bottom of the screen and review the students' beginning letters.

3. Students use the mouse to move the pictures from the bottom of the screen to fill the squares on the bingo board. They click on a picture to select it (notice that the handlebars show in the corners when a picture is selected). They then hold down the mouse on the picture and drag it to move the picture. They let go of the mouse to place the picture in a spreadsheet cell.

4. Students delete pictures they have not moved to the grid.

5. They enter the beginning letter of each picture in its cell by clicking on the cell and typing the letter.

6. Students save their work (this often requires adult assistance) and print out a copy by clicking on the File menu, choosing Print, and selecting OK.

7. The teacher calls out letters, and students use a pencil to place an "x" on the picture that begins with that letter on their printed bingo boards. The first to x-out a row or column wins the game. To get the prize, students must call out their winning row or column, for example, R for rabbit, M for meat, C for cat, W for watermelon, and Y for yogurt.

Extensions

Teachers can modify the *Beginning Letters Bingo* template to create variations.

■ Enter letters on the template and have students find clip art with those letters. To add clip art to the template, click on the Clip Art button.

Figure GS.3.
Insert Clip Art by clicking on the Clip Art icon.

This opens the Insert Clip Art Window (Figure GS.4).

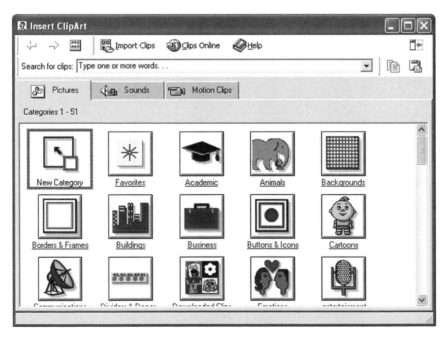

Figure GS.4.
The Clip Art window provides access to hundreds of images.

Students type in the words to describe the picture they want to insert using the correct spelling, or they browse the categories and select a picture by clicking on it. They then click on the Insert Clip button.

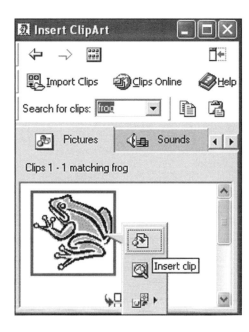

Figure GS.5.
Inserting a clip art image is easy.

The teacher may choose to select and insert appropriate pictures and resize them so that students will only need to move them into place or have students select and insert their own pictures.

- Use all the letters of the alphabet or repeat letters with different pictures.

- Use blends or words containing certain vowel sounds.

- For older students studying vocabulary in language arts, science, or social studies, select bingo words from a chapter or unit of study. The teacher calls out the definition and the students check off the corresponding word. Use it for teaching the classification of the animal kingdom, where in place of BINGO you have the class of fish, bird, amphibian, or mammal. Students choose from a list of animals that they place in the cells.

- Students can make bingo cards to review foreign language vocabulary. The teacher could point to classroom objects, body parts, or hold up a picture, and students identify the word on their bingo card.

Math Facts Review Bingo

Exercise Description

Use the bingo board to review math facts. In the template, students write math problems that add up to 8, 9, 10, 11, and 12 (Figure GS.6). They enter their problems in the given cells on the template, then copy and paste them onto the bingo board. They use the bingo cards to play the game, as the teacher calls out a given cell, for example B1, and an answer. They can use paper markers with the answers on to cover the numbers as the teacher calls them.

	B	C	D	E	F	G	H	I	J	K	L	M	N
1	**Make up math problems, then put them on the Bingo card.**												
2	Make the cell gray after you have put that problem on the Bingo card.												
3													
4	Write math problems where the answer is 8							Write math problems where the answer is 9					
5	4+4=							1.	4+5=				
6	6+2=							2.	6+3=				
7	5+3=							3.	5+4=				
8	7+1=							4.	7+2=				
9													
10	Write math problems where the answer is 10							Write math problems where the answer is 11					
11	5+5=							1.	5+6=				
12	6+4=							2.	7+4=				
13	8+2=							3.	3+8=				
14	9+1=							4.	2+9=				
15													
16	Write math problems where the answer is 12												
17	6+6=												
18	7+5=												
19	3+9=												
20	2+10=												
21													

Figure GS.6. A completed Bingo-Make a Card lesson.

Computer Activity

1. Students open the *Bingo–Make a Card* template and type in their math problems, then enter a different math fact to add up to the given number.

2. Students type in their name for the card that will print. They then copy each problem and paste it onto a cell in the bingo card. To copy a cell, students click on the appropriate cell, and then click on the Edit menu, and on Copy. They then randomly choose a cell in the bingo card, click on it, then they click on the Edit menu, and on Paste. To ensure that each problem is included in the bingo card, they fill the cell with gray after they copy and paste it. To fill a cell with gray, they click on it, then click on the Fill Color button and click on the gray color.

 FillColor Icon

3. When all the cells of the bingo card have been filled, students click on the File menu, and on Save As, and they name their bingo card and save it. They then

click on the File menu, and on Print, and click on OK, to print. Only the bingo cards and markers to place on them will print out (Figure GS.7).

Name:							8	9	10	11	12
	B	I	N	G	O		8	9	10	11	12
1	4+5=	4+4=	5+5=	5+6=	8+2=		8	9	10	11	12
2	6+4=	6+6=	6+3=	5+3=	7+4=		8	9	10	11	12
3	6+2=	7+5=	2+9=	3+8=	9+1=		Cut out these numbers and cover a cell with the right number when it is called.				
4	2+10=	7+2=	7+1=	3+9=	5+4=						

Figure GS.7. A printed Bingo-Make a Card lesson.

Extension

Change the numbers for the math problems. Use subtraction, multiplication, or division instead of addition.

Generate Random Bingo Cards

You can easily make bingo cards with the same text or numbers, placed in random order on the cards. The template *Bingo Cards-Random* on the CD-ROM is a good place to start. Enter the words or math problems that you want to appear on the cards in cells A10 to A29, then give each new card a number in E1 (this generates new random numbers for sorting). Highlight cells A10

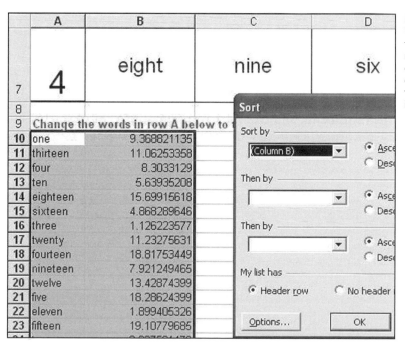

Figure GS.8. Use the Sort function to make numerous different bingo cards that test the same information.

through B29. Click on the Data menu and on Sort, pull down to select by column B (Figure GS.8). This will change the order of the words in column A and their position on the bingo card. Print the card. Only the bingo card, title, and number will print.

To print additional cards, repeat the process with the same words or problems that you entered in A10 to A29. Each bingo card will have these words or problems in a randomly assigned cell. A sample bingo card appears in Figure GS.9.

Title here			Card number here		
	B	**I**	**N**	**G**	**O**
1	one	thirteen	four	ten	eighteen
2	sixteen	three	twenty	fourteen	nineteen
3	twelve	five	eleven	fifteen	two
4	eight	nine	six	seventeen	seven

Figure GS.9.
Create your own bingo cards with the *Bingo Cards-Random* template.

Quick Reference Guide for Using Excel

Personalizing the Toolbar

To add a button to a toolbar: click on the Tools menu, click Customize, and then click the Commands tab. Click on a category, under Categories and click on the command you want on the toolbar under Commands. Hold down your mouse and drag the button to the toolbar at the top of your Excel document. Useful icons for the lessons in this book are the Pattern button and the Fill Color button.

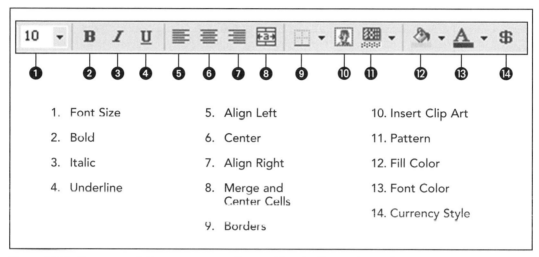

1. Font Size	5. Align Left	10. Insert Clip Art
2. Bold	6. Center	11. Pattern
3. Italic	7. Align Right	12. Fill Color
4. Underline	8. Merge and Center Cells	13. Font Color
	9. Borders	14. Currency Style

Figure QR.1. Here are useful buttons you may like to add to the Formatting toolbar.

Moving around the Spreadsheet

- Use Tab to move to the adjacent cell on the right.

- Use Enter to move to the adjacent cell below.

- Use the Home key to move to the beginning of the row.

- Use the End and right arrow keys to move to the end of the row.

- Use Control and Home to move to the beginning of the spreadsheet.

- Use Control and End to move to the end of the spreadsheet.

Working with Rows and Columns

To resize rows and columns using the mouse: move the pointer over the row or column border. When it changes to a double arrow, drag the border to the position you want.

To resize rows or columns using menus: click on the Format menu and click on Row or Column. Here you can determine the Height or Width or select AutoFit (Figure QR.2).

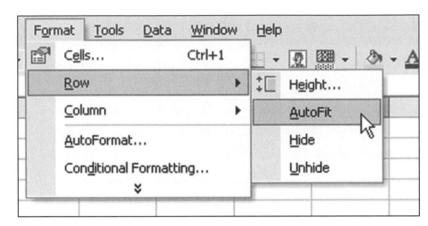

Figure QR.2.
Format and hide rows and columns using the menus.

To automatically format row height by double-clicking: double-click the boundary below the row heading. This makes the row height fit the contents. You can highlight more than one row and change many at a time.

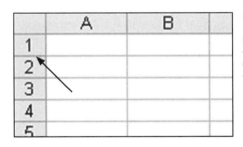

Figure QR.3.
Double-click the boundary below the Row 1 button to automatically fit row height for Row 1.

To automatically format column width: double-click the boundary to the right of the column heading. This makes the column width fit the contents.

To insert rows and columns: first highlight the area next to where you would like to insert the row or column. A row will be inserted above the area you have highlighted and a column will be inserted to the left of the area you have highlighted. Click on the Insert menu and click on Rows or Columns.

To delete rows or columns: highlight the rows or columns you want to delete, click on the Edit menu, and click on Delete.

Formatting a Spreadsheet

To fill a cell with color or pattern: highlight the cell or cells you wish to change. Click on the Format menu, click on Cells and click on the Patterns tab. Click on the arrow next to Pattern to change the pattern and click on the color of your choice. Click on OK. If a mistake is made, click on the Edit menu, and on Undo, or you can change the color and pattern back to plain white. You can also use the Toolbar buttons Fill Color and Pattern.

 Fill Color Icon

 Pattern Icon

To tear away and float the Fill Color or Pattern palettes on the document: click on the Fill Color or Pattern button. Hold down the mouse on its title bar, and drag it onto the document. It will stay open on your document. To hide this floating menu and put it back on the Formatting Toolbar, click on the X in the top right corner.

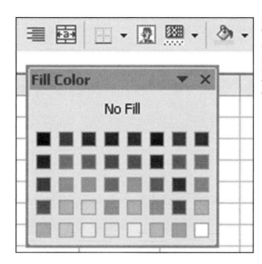

Figure QR.4.
You call pull away the Color and Pattern menus so they float on the worksheet.

To add or remove borders around cells: highlight the cells you want to change. Click on the Format menu and click on Cells, click on the Border tab. Select a line style from the menu on the right, select Outline and Inside, and then click on OK. You can also use the Borders button on the toolbar. Click on the pull-down arrow next to the Borders button and choose your selection from the pop-up menu.

To format a number, highlight the cells you want to change: click on the Format menu, click on Cells, and click on the Number tab. Select the type of number and the number of decimal places you need. You may experience problems formatting fractions, as Excel reads numbers separated with a back slash as dates. To avoid this error, first type in a zero and a space, then the fraction, for example, Type: 0 then space then 1 then backslash then 2 to show 1/2.

To hide a row or column: click on the column or row header to select the entire column or row. Click on Format, then on Column or Row, and choose Hide. To reveal a hidden column, click on the headers of the columns before and after it, click on the Format menu, choose Column, then Unhide. Do the same to unhide a hidden row.

Managing Cells

To make menu options available: click in a cell.

To delete a cell: highlight the cell you want to delete, click on the Edit menu, and click on Delete.

Use AutoInsert to insert text from a cell above in the same column: Choose Pick from List by right-clicking the cell. Excel automatically generates this list, and you make a selection by clicking on it.

To Fill Down or Fill Right: highlight the cells containing the data you want to duplicate. Hold down the Ctrl key and press D to Fill Down or R to Fill Right. You can also drag cell contents across or down by holding down the mouse on the corner of a cell and dragging. The contents of that cell will be duplicated in other cells that you highlight (Figure QR.5). You can fill cells with data from another cell. You can also fill cells with a repeating pattern from highlighted cells. You can fill cells with numbers, dates, or times in increments that you stipulate, and you can also fill formulas.

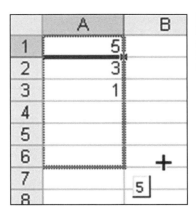

Figure QR.5. Drag the corner of a cell to copy its contents to other cells.

To sort spreadsheet data: select the rows or columns you want to sort. Click on the Data menu and choose Sort. If you are sorting more than one row or column, you can select the order in which to sort them.

To add a comment: click on the Insert menu, click on Comment, or right-click the cell and click on Insert Comment (Figure QR.6). The worksheet author's name appears on the comment, but you can delete this if you wish, and add a comment.

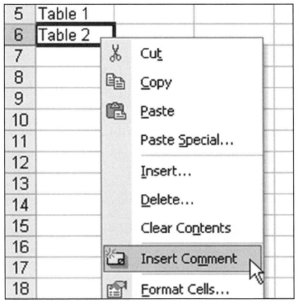

Figure QR.6. Right-click and choose Insert Comment from the pop-up menu.

To protect a worksheet: remember that by default, cells on Excel spreadsheets are locked. Unlock cells that you want students to change before you enable protection, or you will lock all the cells in the spreadsheet, making changes impossible. To Lock or Unlock Cells, highlight the cells you want to affect, click on the Format menu, select Cells, select the Protection tab, and check or clear the Locked check box. Next, turn on protection by clicking on the Tools menu, select Protection, then Protect Sheet. To move between unlocked cells on a protected worksheet, click an unlocked cell, and then press Tab.

Placing Clip Art

To insert clip art: click on the Insert menu, Picture, and then Clip Art. Or, click on the Insert Clip Art button on the Drawing toolbar. Type in the word for the item you are searching for, click on the picture you want to insert, and click on the Insert Clip button. If you don't have very many pictures available, you may not have installed Clip Gallery when you installed Microsoft Office. To do this, consult your help menu and find instructions to "Install or remove individual components of Microsoft Office or Microsoft Excel."

To download pictures from Microsoft Office Online's Clip Art and Media page: click on the Insert Clip Art button on the Drawing toolbar, and click on the Clips Online button. This should automatically open up the Clip Art and Media page, Microsoft's online clip art page for licensed Office users. From this page you can search for pictures by key word or browse by category. Click on the button below the picture to add or remove it from your selection basket. You can click Review basket to see everything you have selected. Click Download on the menu bar when you have finished selecting your pictures and follow the instructions. The pictures are downloaded in a format that can be directly imported into your Clip Gallery or Clip Organizer.

To duplicate a picture: click on the picture, hold down the Ctrl key and drag to where you want the picture to go, or hold down the Ctrl button and press D once. Continue doing this until you have the number of duplicates you want.

To resize a picture: click on the picture to select it, and the four handlebars in the corners of the picture will show. Hold down the mouse on one of them and drag.

To move a picture: click in the middle of it, hold down the mouse, and drag.

To modify a picture: click on the picture to select it. Click on the Draw toolbar at the bottom of the screen. Click Draw, then click Ungroup (Or, left-click, and select Ungroup from the pop-up menu). You will notice that each part of the picture becomes a separate picture that can be deleted, moved, colored, et cetera. You can remove the rectangle around the picture in this way. To regroup the pieces of the picture, click on the pointer arrow in the draw menu and hold down your mouse and drag it over the picture to select all the parts, then click on the Draw menu and click on Regroup. Sometimes it's necessary to Ungroup and Regroup a picture when you want to change it, such as rotate it. Ungrouping and regrouping changes the format of the picture and gives you more options.

Making Charts

To make a chart: highlight the cells containing data you want to show on your chart. Click on Insert and click on Chart. The Wizard will allow you to choose the type of chart, select series in rows or columns, label x and y axes. To remove the word "Series" on the chart and replace it with the column headings, make sure that Series in Columns is checked. When you click on Finish, the computer will generate a graph.

To edit a chart or graph: right-click on the chart and click on Chart Options. The Chart Options window will open up.

To change the color of a slice on a pie chart or a bar in a bar graph: double-click on the piece you want to change. This will bring up the Format Data Point dialog box where you can then select your color, or format your data labels. Alternately, you can get to this dialog box by clicking Format then Selected Data Point.

Using Formulas and Functions

Formulas make calculations with cell data. Select the cell where you want the formula to go. Type an equal sign, = to let the computer know that you're entering a formula. Be very careful about where you click next, as this will become part of your formula. If you make a mistake, backspace or delete the formula and start again. If this does not work, press the Escape key. Type in the formula. Example =A1+A2 (The cell address can be typed in or it can be entered by clicking on that cell). Math symbols on computer include:

- add +
- subtract –
- multiply *
- divide /
- exponent ^

To show or hide formulas on the worksheet: open the Tools menu, select Options, and click the View tab. Add a check mark next to Formulas to show formulas. Remember, formulas will always show up in the Formula bar (at the top of the window), when you click on the cell containing that formula.

To insert a function, or ready-made formula: open the Insert menu and click on Function. Select the function you want, then highlight the words in parentheses (arguments) and replace them with the addresses of cells containing the data you want in the calculation. Press enter and the formula is placed in the cell.

- To add cell contents: =SUM(number1,number2,…)
- To multiply cell contents: =PRODUCT(number1,number2,…)
- To average cell contents: =AVERAGE(number1,number2,…)

- To find the maximum value for a set of scores =MAX(B1:B6)

- To find the minimum value for a set of scores =MIN(B4:C4)

- To find the square of a number: =SQRT(number)

- To generate a random number between 0 and 1: =RAND()

- To generate a random number between 1 and 20: =RAND()*20

- To round a number up, away from zero, to the nearest integer: =ROUNDUP(A1,1)

- To respond to student input if they answer a particular answer, e.g., 7, =IF(B1=7,"Well done!","Try again.")

- To respond to student input with two conditions to be satisfied =IF(AND(H11="7",A11=0),"Well done!","Try again.")

  This means if both H11 = 7 and A11 = 0, then fill in Well done! Otherwise, fill in Try again.

- To count cells containing a certain word: =COUNTIF(B1:B5,"Well done!")

- To insert a hyperlink in a cell =HYPERLINK("http://www.google.com")

Note: Functions must refer to data in a different cell or you will get a circular reference error message.

Printing a Spreadsheet

To set Print range: first highlight the area you want to print. Click on the File menu, click on Print Area, and choose Set Print Area. It is important to do this to avoid the possibility of printing the entire spreadsheet. Click on the File menu and click on Print Preview or click on the Print Preview button on the toolbar. Click on Close to return to Normal View of the spreadsheet.

To set Display Options: click on the File menu and click on Page Setup and click on the Sheet tab. Column and Row headings and Gridlines will not automatically show up on printed copies. To print row and column headings, check Row and column headings. To print the grid, add a check mark next to Gridlines.

 Print Preview Icon

To add a header or footer: click on the View menu, click on Header or Footer. A dialogue box will appear. Click on Custom Header or Custom Footer. Type in the desired text. Click on OK.

Standards by Lesson

SPREADSHEET LESSON		STANDARDS					
		ISTE NETS•S Standards	NCTE English Language Arts	NCTM Math	NAS Science	NCSS Social Studies	ACTFL Foreign Language
I	Creating Bingo Cards	1, 3		1			
Kindergarten							
1	Counting to 10	1, 3		1			
2	Classifying Nouns	1, 3	3				
First Grade							
3	Counting on a Grid	1, 3		1, 2			
4	March Weather Watch	4, 5		1, 4, 5, 10	A1	IIIf	
5	Recognizing Patterns	2		2			
6	Pets Survey	4, 5		5			
Second Grade							
7	Math Problems with 5, 7, and 9	3		1, 3, 6			
8	Money to Spend	6		1, 6, 9			
9	Finding the Rule	6		1, 2, 6			
10	Change for a Bill	6		1, 6			
11	Apple-Tasting Survey	4	7	5			
12	Bats or Birds?	3	1, 4, 8		C1		
Third Grade							
13	Secret Message: Pledge of Allegiance	1, 3		3		VIb, d	
14	Plot the Points on a Grid	1, 3, 6		3		IIIa	
15	Creating a Multiplication Table	1, 3		1, 2			
16	Budgeting Money	1, 3, 6		1, 6, 9			
17	Counting Colored Candies	1, 3, 4, 5		5, 9, 10			
18	Classifying Vertebrates	1, 2, 3, 4, 5			C1		
19	Brainstorming and Organizing Ideas	6	5			VIa, e	
20	Designing Place Cards	3	6	3			

continued

NATIONAL EDUCATIONAL TECHNOLOGY STANDARDS

1. Basic Operations and Concepts
2. Social, Ethical, and Human Issues
3. Technology Productivity Tools
4. Technology Communications Tools
5. Technology Research Tools
6. Technology Problem-solving and Decision-making Tools

Standards by Lesson *continued*

SPREADSHEET LESSON		ISTE NETS•S Standards	NCTE English Language Arts	NCTM Math	NAS Science	NCSS Social Studies	ACTFL Foreign Language
Fourth Grade							
21	Word Search	1, 3	3				
22	Magic Square	6		1, 2			
23	My Measurements	6		4, 5	C1		
24	Formulas for Converters	3		1, 2, 4			
25	Visualizing Fractions	3		1, 3			
26	Music Survey	4		5, 7	A1		
27	States and Capitals	3				IIIa, c	
Fifth Grade							
28	Science Dictionary	3			B		
29	Decimals and Negatives	6		1, 3			
30	Finding Prime Numbers	3		1, 2, 3			
31	U.S. Weather Chart	3, 4		3, 5, 6, 10	D	IIIf	
32	Concept Maps: Fairy Tales	3, 4	5				
33	Planning a Road Trip	6	8			IIIa, b, c, d	
Sixth Grade							
34	Colored Candies: Ratio, Percentage, and Estimation	4		5, 6, 9, 10			
35	Foreign Language Dictionary	3					1.2
36	Using Formulas to Calculate Equations	3		2, 6			
37	Travel Slideshow	1, 2, 3, 6		2, 6			1.2; 1.3; 3.1; 3.2; 5.1
38	Analyzing Complex Patterns	3		2			
39	Probability with Coins and Dice	3, 6		5			
40	Comparing Countries	4, 5		2		III, VI, VII	

SUBJECT AREAS FOR MATH STANDARDS

1. Number and Operations
2. Algebra
3. Geometry
4. Measurement
5. Data Analysis And Probability
6. Problem Solving
7. Reasoning And Proof
8. Communication
9. Connections
10. Representation

Scope and Sequence Chart of Spreadsheet Skills

COMPUTER SKILLS	K	1	2	3	4	5	6
Charts							
Insert a chart, select a chart type		X	X	X	X	X	X
Give a chart or graph a title		X	X	X	X	X	X
Change the color on a pie chart or bar graph				X	X	X	X
Resize and move charts				X	X	X	X
Select non-adjacent data to chart using Ctrl key					X	X	X
Format a Chart					X	X	X
Right-click on a chart and edit it						X	X
Delete series on a chart or graph							X
Document							
Open a document, use Save As		X	X	X	X	X	X
Hide or unhide rows/columns			X	X	X	X	X
View toolbars						X	X
Editing							
Insert text or numbers in a cell	X	X	X	X	X	X	X
Insert or delete columns and rows			X	X	X	X	X
Resize columns and rows			X	X	X	X	X
Insert and Delete cells			X	X	X	X	X
Enter numbers using the number pad			X	X	X	X	X
Enter numbers, plus signs, and equal signs			X	X	X	X	X
Drag and drop contents of a cell			X	X	X	X	X
Edit a spreadsheet and use Undo				X	X	X	X
Extend contents of a cell using Fill Right or Fill Down				X	X	X	X
Show/Hide formulas or data				X	X	X	X
Delete text				X	X	X	X
Copy and Paste text				X	X	X	X
Copy Spreadsheet cells using Ctrl, drag, and drop				X	X	X	X

continued

Scope and Sequence Chart of Spreadsheet Skills *continued*

COMPUTER SKILLS	K	1	2	3	4	5	6
Formatting							
Change font type, size, color		X	X	X	X	X	X
Fill cell with color or pattern		X	X	X	X	X	X
Format Borders			X	X	X	X	X
Format a number as a decimal, fraction, currency			X	X	X	X	X
Wrap text in a cell				X	X	X	X
Add or remove cell borders					X	X	X
Underline Text						X	X
Format numbers as fixed numbers						X	X
Formulas							
Create a formula			X	X	X	X	X
Use ready-made formulas			X	X	X	X	X
Fill a formula down or right			X	X	X	X	X
Show Formulas or Data			X	X	X	X	X
Calculate Averages or Percentages using formulas						X	X
Insert and generalize formula							X
Format numbers as percentages using formulas							X
Functions							
Use AutoSum function							X
Generate random numbers and use COUNTIF function							X
Use function to calculate the value of an absolute							X
Graphics							
Insert clip art, move it, resize it, duplicate it, delete it	X	X	X	X	X	X	X
Select a picture	X	X	X	X	X	X	X
Draw basic shapes		X	X	X	X	X	X
Use the line and arrow tools			X	X	X	X	X
Insert a picture from Microsoft's Clip Art Web page			X	X	X	X	X
Insert, resize, and move digital photographs			X	X	X	X	X
Modify, move, and format WordArt				X	X	X	X
Flip WordArt horizontally and vertically				X	X	X	X

continued

Scope and Sequence Chart of Spreadsheet Skills *continued*

COMPUTER SKILLS	K	1	2	3	4	5	6
Internet							
Copy and paste a picture or text from a Web page				X	X	X	X
Move between Spreadsheets and Browser				X	X	X	X
Copy and paste a Web page address (URL)					X	X	X
Use Internet Map Service						X	X
Search Internet							X
Navigation							
Move around spreadsheet using the mouse, Enter, Tab			X	X	X	X	X
Move between sheets on a Spreadsheet					X	X	X
Printing							
Use Print Preview, print a document	X	X	X	X	X	X	X
Set print area				X	X	X	X
Other							
Insert the degree symbol		X	X	X	X	X	X
Use Calculator Tool			X	X	X	X	X
Sort alphabetically and numerically				X	X	X	X
Add note							X
Automatically insert day of the week, months							X
Insert spreadsheet into a slide show							X

Kindergarten Lessons

1. **Counting to 10** (MATH)

2. **Classifying Nouns** (LANGUAGE ARTS)

1. Counting to 10

Lesson Description

Kindergarten students duplicate animal pictures and place them on the spreadsheet grid in the appropriate cell as they count from 1 to 10. They practice reading the numbers, which are on the *Counting to 10* template and may be read aloud as a class. One of each picture has already been inserted on the spreadsheet template. The pictures have been sized appropriately, so students need only learn how to duplicate and move graphics to complete the assignment.

Higher-Order Thinking Skills	Spreadsheet Skills Practiced	Subject Areas and Standards Addressed
Connect visual representations and the abstract concept of numbers	Entering text in a cell Duplicating and moving pictures Printing a document	NETS•S: 1, 3 Mathematics: 1

Computer Activity

1. Students open the *Counting to 10* template.

Count to 10		Name:										
1												
2												
3												
4												
5												
6												
7												
8												
9												
10												

Figure 1.1.
The *Counting to 10* template.

2. The teacher demonstrates how to select a picture by clicking on it so that the handlebars show, and how to duplicate the selected picture by holding down the Control key and pressing D. The duplicate picture appears on the screen.

3. Students select the duplicate picture by clicking on it and move it by holding the mouse down on the picture, dragging it, and letting go at the appropriate position. Note: depending on the version of Excel that you are using, you may get an error message if you double click on a picture or if you click on a picture and try to enter text or numbers. If this happens, press the Esc or escape key on the upper left corner of the keyboard.

4. When the assignment has been completed, the student enters his or her name and prints the document by clicking on the File menu and selecting Print.

5. Students look at the hard copy as they answer the following questions:

   ■ Are there more dogs or horses?

   ■ How do you know that? (Students may refer to the larger number, 7>3, or the fact that more squares on the grid are taken up by the bigger group.)

   ■ Which number is the largest?

   ■ Which number is the smallest?

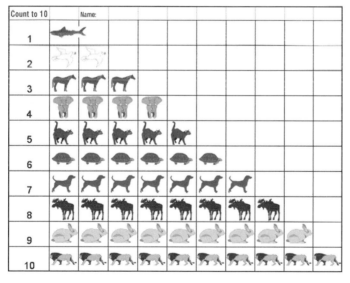

Figure 1.2. Completed Counting to 10 assignment.

Extension Assignment

Students who easily complete the above assignment can open the *Counting 2* template. Here they enter the numbers 11 to 20 and duplicate pictures to represent those numbers.

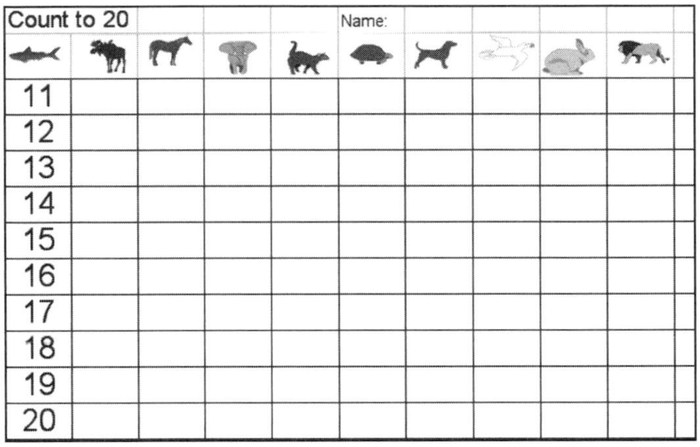

Count to 20					Name:						
11											
12											
13											
14											
15											
16											
17											
18											
19											
20											

Figure 1.3.
The *Counting 2* template.

2. Classifying Nouns

Lesson Description

Students begin to distinguish between the different types of words that make up our language. They classify nouns into the categories of People, Places, and Things by dragging pictures into the appropriate cell. They then find their own pictures to add to each category.

Higher-Order Thinking Skills	Spreadsheet Skills Practiced	Subject Areas and Standards Addressed
Apply understanding of the concept of nouns and the vocabulary words people, places, and things Select pictures and organize them Classify new nouns using images Choose pictures Create new categories with original ideas	Insert and resize clip art Move clip art	NETS•S: 1, 3 English Language Arts: 3

Computer Activity

Students open the *Nouns* template (Figure 2.1).

1. They click on an image and drag it to place it in the correct position.

2. When all the pictures have been moved, they click on the Insert Clip Art button. They click on a category, for example *animals*, click on the picture they want to insert, and click on Insert Clip. They then hold down the mouse on the corner of the picture, grabbing the handlebar, and drag from corner to corner, to make it smaller. They then drag the picture to its category.

3. Click on the Print Preview button to check that this document will print on one page.

Print Preview Icon

4. Print the document. Students write beginning letters on the hard copy underneath each picture after it prints out.

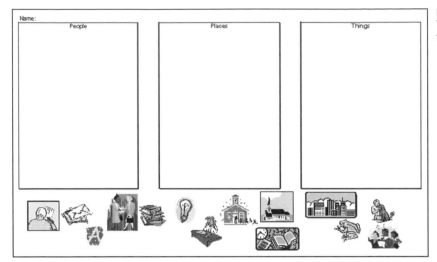

Figure 2.1.
The *Nouns*
template.

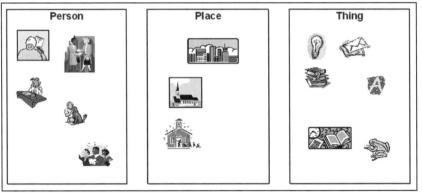

Figure 2.2.
A completed
Nouns lesson.

Instructions for the teacher: To make the rectangles taller, first highlight a row inside the rectangle. Click on the row heading, click on the Insert menu, then click on Rows. Repeat this step until the rectangle is tall enough. Save the modified template.

Extension

After listing words in cells below the categories, have students drag them to the appropriate place. For example, list each of the nouns in the previous picture and have students match them with the pictures. Alternatively, require students to use only words as a way to reinforce reading skills.

Modify the *Categories* template to get students to classify other things. For example, students could classify animals that walk, animals that fly, and animals that swim, or animals that live in different habitats. Add clip art to get them started. The template could also be used with words that begin with a certain letter, or words containing a certain vowel sound. After completing the required lesson, students open the *Categories* template, define their own three categories, and find pictures to help distinguish among them.

First-Grade Lessons

3. **Counting on a Grid** (MATH)

    - Counting to 100

    - Counting by 2s, 3s, and 5s

    - Counting Large Numbers

4. **March Weather Watch** (MATH, SCIENCE, LANGUAGE ARTS)

    - March Calendar

    - Pictograph of March Weather

    - Bar Graph of March Weather

5. **Recognizing Patterns** (MATH)

6. **Pets Survey** (MATH)

3. Counting on a Grid

Lesson Description

Students use a spreadsheet grid to count in the following three exercises: Counting to 100; Counting by 2s, 3s, and 5s; and Counting Large Numbers. Relationships between numbers and number patterns become evident as students work on the activities. They become aware of counting by 10s in columns, and they notice that the first digit remains the same in rows and that the second digit remains the same in columns.

Higher-Order Thinking Skills	Spreadsheet Skills Practiced	Subject Areas and Standards Addressed
Connect visual representations and the abstract concept of numbers Use visual cues to perceive order Recognize patterns, analyze them, organize numbers on the number line Select multiples of numbers, and explain where they intersect	Enter text in a cell and become familiar with the grid format Move around the spreadsheet using the arrow and Tab keys Correct errors Fill cells with color or pattern Underline text Change the color of text Save a document	NETS•S: 1, 3 Mathematics: 1, 2

Counting to 100

Exercise Description

Students practice counting to 100 by counting candies, counting to the 100th day of school, counting down from 100 to 0 days until a special event, and other such activities. Teachers may find it useful to print the grid without numbers and have students fill in the numbers on a paper copy before starting the computer exercise. This gives students further practice writing and organizing the numbers.

As students become aware of patterns in the number system, many of them begin to enter numbers going down rather than across because they find this is faster. The patterns make it easy to check for mistakes as the teacher scans the columns and rows. Students often correct their own mistakes as they read out the numbers they have entered and then notice that they mistakenly skipped some numbers. It is clear to see that a number is missing as the pattern is disrupted if, for example, the row does not end in a multiple of 10.

1	2	3	4	5	6	7	8	9	10
11	12	13	14	15	16	17	18	19	20
21	22	23	24	25	26	27	28	29	30
31	32	33	34	35	36	37	38	39	40
41	42	43	44	45	46	47	48	49	50
51	52	53	54	55	56	57	58	59	60
61	62	63	64	65	66	67	68	69	70
71	72	73	74	75	76	77	78	79	80
81	82	83	84	85	86	87	88	89	90
91	92	93	94	95	96	97	98	99	100

Figure 3.1.
A completed
Counting to 100
lesson.

Computer Activity

1. Open the *Counting to 100* template. Borders, font, size, and print area have been preset.

2. Enter the numbers 1 to 100 in cells A1 through J10. Use the Tab and arrow keys to move around the spreadsheet.

3. Correct any errors by clicking on the cell with the mistake and editing or retyping in the entry bar.

4. Save the document, by clicking on the File menu and on Save.

Extensions

- Students print out their 100s chart and, using the hard copy, circle adjacent cells that add up to a given number, such as 35. Numbers they would circle that add up to 35 could include the following:

  2, 12, 21   17, 18   8, 9, 18

- The printed number chart can be used to find the sum of numbers. For example,

  73+10 =   84−10 =   78+20 =   40+32 =   55+9=   34−9 =

- Students who have completed the lesson and printed it out can delete all the numbers on the spreadsheet and, starting at 101, they can count to 200.

- After deleting the numbers, students could use the same grid and begin with a given number, for example 25, and count by 5s (or 3s, or any other number).

- Students who have problems adding numbers can use an online calculator to count in multiples. The National Council of Teachers of Mathematics has a Web page entitled "Learning about Number Relationships and Properties of Numbers: Using Calculators and Hundred Boards: Patterns to 100 and Beyond." Students who have Web access can do the activity online at the following Web address: http://standards.nctm.org/document/eexamples/chap4/4.5/index.htm/.

- Students delete all numbers from the 100s chart and fill cells to make patterns of three, four, or five cells. They can fill a cell with color or pattern. They copy and paste the shading and can make a grid with vertical, horizontal, or diagonal stripes.

- Older students can use the template from this lesson to make a chart to count to 100 in a different base, such as base 5 or base 2. Students could begin with base 10 and cut, paste, delete, and change numbers to get the other bases. A sample of base 5 appears in Figure 3.2, and a sample of base 2 appears in Figure 3.3.

Name: Jane D.						Base 10	
Base 5							
1	2	3	4	10		5	5^1
11	12	13	14	20		10	
21	22	23	24	30		15	
31	32	33	34	40		20	
41	42	43	44	100		25	5^2
101	102	103	104	110		30	
111	112	113	114	120		35	
121	122	123	124	130		40	
131	132	133	134	140		45	
141	142	143	144	200		50	

Figure 3.2. Counting with base 5.

Name:		Base10	
Base Two			
1	10	2	2^1
11	100	4	2^2
101	110	6	
111	1000	8	2^3
1001	1010	10	
1011	1100	12	
1101	1110	14	
1111	10000	16	2^4
10001	10010	18	
10011	10100	20	

Figure 3.3. Counting with base 2.

Counting by 2s, 3s, and 5s

Exercise Description

First-grade students learn to count by 2s, 3s, and 5s. Students who have completed the number chart change the fill color, fill pattern, and text to highlight the multiples of a number.

Computer Activity

Before students begin this activity, make sure the Formatting toolbar is showing. Click on the View menu and on Toolbars, and on Formatting. It helps if the following buttons are showing on the formatting toolbar: Fill Color, Font Color, and Pattern. If the pattern button isn't showing, click on the View menu, click on Toolbars, and choose Customize. Click on the Format category, and scroll down to find the Pattern button. Use the mouse to drag it to the Formatting toolbar at the top of the document.

Pattern Icon

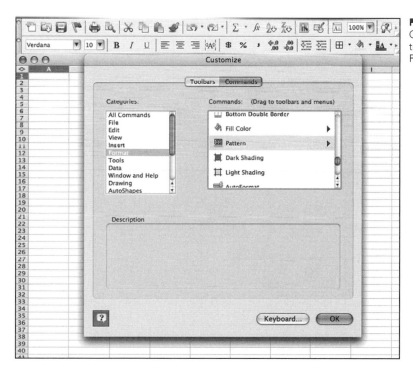

Figure 3.4.
Customize the toolbar with the Pattern button.

1.   Students open their saved 100s chart.

2.   To tear away the Fill Color palette, select the Paint Bucket or Fill Color button on the Formatting toolbar, click on the arrow next to it, hold down the mouse on the title or moving bar, and drag it onto the document so that it is easily accessible.

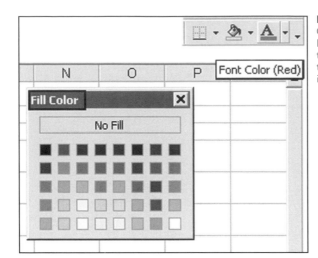

Figure 3.5.
Grab the top of the Fill Color palette to tear it away from the toolbar, making it float on the page.

3. Starting from 0, students count by 2s and fill those cells with red. They select a cell by clicking on it, then change the fill color by selecting the color of choice on the Fill Color palette. To fill a cell with pattern, click on the cell to select it, then click on the Pattern button on the Formatting toolbar. The Pattern palette can also be torn away so that it floats on the document, by holding down the mouse on its moving or title bar, and dragging it onto the document.

1	2	3	4	5	6	7	8	9	10
11	12	13	14	15	16	17	18	19	20
21	22	23	24	25	26	27	28	29	30
31	32	33	34	35	36	37	38	39	40
41	42	43	44	45	46	47	48	49	50
51	52	53	54	55	56	57	58	59	60
61	62	63	64	65	66	67	68	69	70
71	72	73	74	75	76	77	78	79	80
81	82	83	84	85	86	87	88	89	90
91	92	93	94	95	96	97	98	99	100

Count by 2s	(Fill with red)			
Count by 5s	(Underline)			
Count by 3s	(Fill with pattern)			

Figure 3.6.
A completed Counting by 2s, 3s, and 5s lesson.

4. Students count by 5s, starting with 0, and underline the number in each of those cells by selecting the text and clicking on the Underline (U) button in the toolbar.

5. Students count by 3s, starting with 0, and fill each of those cells with a pattern.

6. Students may change the color of the text in a selected cell by selecting the appropriate cell and clicking on the Font Color button, then on a color.

Extension

This exercise may be modified for more advanced students, who count by multiples of higher numbers.

Counting Large Numbers

Exercise Description

Students who have learned to count larger numbers can complete grids using those higher numbers. They also count forward by 10s or count backward by 10s.

Computer Activity

Students open the *Counting Large Numbers* template and fill in the missing numbers on the grids or pieces of grids.

Figure 3.7. The *Counting Large Numbers* template with formulas showing.

Fill in the missing numbers:

451	=B3+1	=C3+1	=D3+1						=B3+9
	=C3+10		=C4+3						
=B3+20		=B5+2				=B5+6	=B5+7		=B5+9
			=E3+30				=B3+38		

Count by 10s:

610			=B9+30	=B9+40				=B9+80	=B9+90
						=B9+160			
	=B9+210			=B9+250					=B9+290

Count back by 10s:

424			=B14-30					
				=B14-150				

Extensions

- Starting with 451, students count by 2s, filling every other cell with color. They look at the pattern made by the color and answer the question "How would the outcome be different if you started filling color at 452?" (There would still be columns of color alternating with columns without color, but the color would move one column to the right.)

- Students count forward by 5s or another denomination in place of 10s, and count backward by that number as well.

- The teacher can change the starting number for each of the grids on the template. Formulas have been entered in the cells, so all the other numbers on the template will change when the starting number is changed. In this way a new lesson has been generated for students, who then complete the exercise as described above.

  To change the first number on each of the grids or pieces of grid, the teacher or student simply enters a different number in each of the cells containing numbers, for example B3, B9, B14, C18. If the first numbers are changed, the other numbers on the template will change. If the formulas are showing in the cells, the teacher then highlights all the cells, clicks on the Tools menu, selects Options, clicks on the View tab, and removes the check mark next to Formulas. Students now have a different worksheet to complete. In this way the teacher can easily and quickly generate similar worksheets to give additional practice to students who struggle with counting or for students who finish the initial lesson quickly.

  The exercise could then be saved as "Counting with Formulas 2." Students could complete it on the computer or it could be printed it out and they could finish it with a pencil.

For More Advanced Users: Cells were locked so that a formula could not be deleted in error, but if you wanted to change the way this exercise is set up, you need to unlock the cells, as described on the template.

4. March Weather Watch

Lesson Description

This lesson is divided into three separate exercises. The initial exercise allows students to create a March calendar. They input the appropriate days and important dates, and then save and print the calendars. The hard copy is used for recording daily weather and temperature. At the end of the month, students open the saved March calendar, enter symbols for the weather and daily temperatures, and print again. Students number the days of the month and divide them up into seven-day weeks. Students use units of measurement to record temperatures and compare them day-by-day. The class discusses what the weather is normally like in their town for the month of March, and explores how to monitor it. March is a good month for noticing some changes in the wintry weather. Students use a thermometer to gather weather data, then plot the data they have collected on graphs and interpret their findings.

The second exercise allows students to create a pictograph based on the weather data they collected. In the third exercise, students create a bar graph using the same data. Students note the weather changes and discuss what causes them.

Higher-Order Thinking Skills	Spreadsheet Skills Practiced	Subject Areas and Standards Addressed
Create a calendar	Enter text in a cell	NETS•S: 4, 5
Plan how to record daily weather (with whole class)	Enter data students have collected	Mathematics: 1, 4, 5, 10
Apply knowledge of weather to create a picto-graph and a bar graph	Add, resize, and move clip art	Science: A1
	Duplicate pictures	Social Studies: IIIf
	Insert the degree symbol	
	Fill cells with color	
	Print a document	

March Calendar

Exercise Description

Students create a March calendar by entering the days of the week, adding important events, and illustrating with clip art. They use a printout of the March calendar to record weather information for the month, which they enter on their computer file.

Computer Activity

1. Before the beginning of March, students open the *Calendar* template.

2. Students enter the names of the days of the week and number the dates in the month. They write in events such as the beginning of a new season, the start of vacation, holidays, and birthdays.

3. Students insert clip art to illustrate each event (see the "Quick Reference Guide for Using Excel" at the beginning of this book for instructions on working with clip art).

4. Students save and print their calendars.

5. Throughout the month of March students record the weather each day on the hard copy of their calendars. They note whether it is sunny, partly cloudy, cloudy, rainy, or snowy by drawing a symbol onto the calendar they printed out.

6. Students observe the temperature each day on a thermometer and note it on the calendar printout.

7. At the end of the month, students open the saved calendar for March and add clip art to describe each day's weather.

8. They enter the temperature for each day of the month (see directions for adding the degree symbol).

9. When the lesson has been completed, students save again and print a copy.

Adding the Degree Symbol

To put in the degree symbol, students could highlight and copy the one on the template. Students who find this difficult can draw in the degree symbol after they print.

To use keyboard shortcuts to insert the degree symbol, hold down Alt and press 0176, release the Alt key, and the symbol appears where your cursor was on the document.

To use the Character Map to insert the degree symbol:

1. Click on the Start menu, select Programs, then Accessories, System Tools, and Character Map.

2. Select Arial to match the font and click on the degree symbol (°).

3. Click on Select and Copy, then close the Character Map.

4. Paste the symbol on your calendar by clicking where you need to insert it, holding down the Edit menu, and selecting Paste.

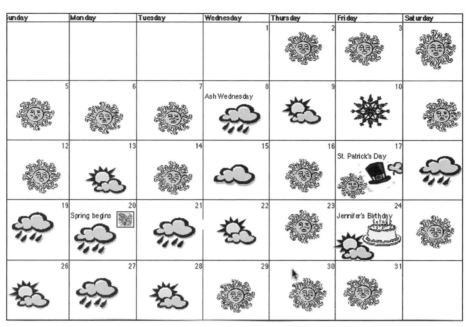

Figure 4.1. A completed March Calendar lesson.

Pictograph of March Weather

Exercise Description

After monitoring the weather for a month and completing the March weather calendar, students create a pictograph using symbols from clip art. Symbols are duplicated the correct number of times to complete the pictograph. Students learn how data may be represented graphically.

Computer Activity

1. Students open the *Weather Pictograph* template.

2. They find pictures to describe the weather for the month, including sunny, partly cloudy, cloudy, rainy, and snowy (see directions in the previous section for adding clip art).

3. They duplicate to get the appropriate number of symbols for each type of weather. For instance, if March had three sunny days, they should place three sun symbols in the Sunny column (see directions in the previous section for duplicating a picture).

4. Teachers may edit the template if desired (to add a "windy" column, for instance), but first the cells must be unlocked. (Some cells have been locked to prevent students from deleting information on the template.) To unlock cells, highlight all the cells in the spreadsheet. Click on the Tools menu, click on Protection, and on Unprotect Sheet.

5. Students save the document and print it.

6. The class discusses the findings.

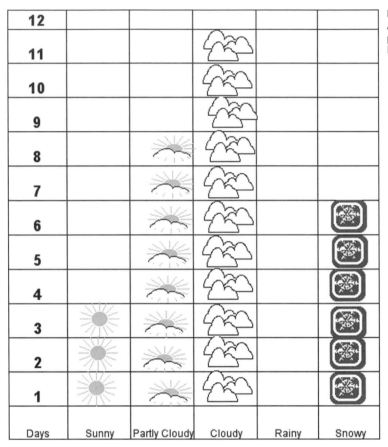

12					
11			⛅⛅		
10			⛅⛅		
9			⛅		
8		☀️	⛅⛅		
7		☀️	⛅⛅		
6		☀️	⛅⛅		❄️
5		☀️	⛅⛅		❄️
4		☀️	⛅		❄️
3	☀️	☀️	⛅⛅		❄️
2	☀️	☀️	⛅⛅		❄️
1	☀️	☀️	⛅		❄️
Days	Sunny	Partly Cloudy	Cloudy	Rainy	Snowy

Figure 4.2.
A completed pictograph of March weather.

Bar Graph of March Weather

Description

Students make a bar graph using the data from the previous March lessons and learn that information can be conveyed in different ways.

Computer Activity

1. Students open the *Weather Bar Graph* template.

2. They make sure that the Formatting toolbar is showing. To show the toolbar, students can go to the View menu and click on Toolbars then Formatting.

3. Students select the cells that they want to fill with gray by holding down the mouse and dragging the cursor over those cells.

4. When the cells are selected, they choose the fill color by clicking on the Fill Color button and clicking on the color gray.

5. The total number in each weather category can be added to get a total number of days for all the weather categories in the month. This equation is entered into empty cells in the spreadsheet. Ask students whether this total matches the number of days in March. Why or why not?

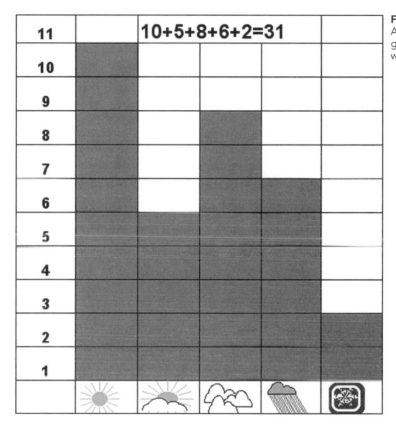

Figure 4.3.
A completed bar graph of March weather.

Extension

Students make a bar graph showing how many medals were won by the top 10 countries in the Olympic games. They open the *Olympics Bar Graph* template and fill cells to make the bar graph.

5. Recognizing Patterns

Lesson Description

Students begin by repeating simple color or number patterns on a hundreds chart. They look for patterns on the diagonal and from top to bottom. They add numbers to make this a number pattern. The extension allows them to make patterns with colors, letters, and shapes. Students who struggle with that can continue to generate patterns with colors or numbers on the *Patterns* template. A blank copy of the template can be printed for students to color and write on. The *Patterns* template may be used for number or letter patterns. Students can make patterns with three or four different colors.

Before the lesson, tear away the Fill Color palette at each computer station by clicking on it on the Formatting toolbar, holding down the mouse on the title bar, and dragging it onto the document.

Higher-Order Thinking Skills	Spreadsheet Skills Practiced	Subject Areas and Standards Addressed
Identify the pattern parts, predict what comes next, and describe it Use a productivity tool to solve a problem Create an original pattern	Enter text in cells Fill cells with color Draw, resize, move basic shapes	NETS•S: 2 Mathematics: 2

Computer Activity

1. Students open the *Patterns* template (Figure 5.1).

2. Students click on a cell, then select a color on the Fill Color palette. They continue in this way to build a pattern.

3. Remind students that if they're typing in a cell, they can't access the fill colors. Click on a different cell to get out of typing mode, click back on the cell whose color you want to change to select it. To remove a color from a cell, simply select the cell with color and click on No Fill on the Fill Color palette. To delete a number, click on the cell and press the delete key. If you are stuck in a cell, press the Esc key on the keyboard.

4. When students have completed a color pattern, they insert numbers that correspond with the colors, such as 1 for blue, 2 for red, 3 for yellow. Ask students if they notice any patterns in the numbers from top to bottom and on the diagonal.

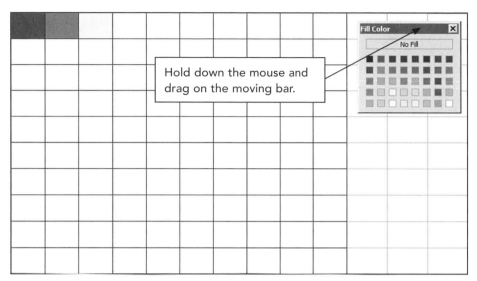

Figure 5.1. Patterns help students understand math concepts.

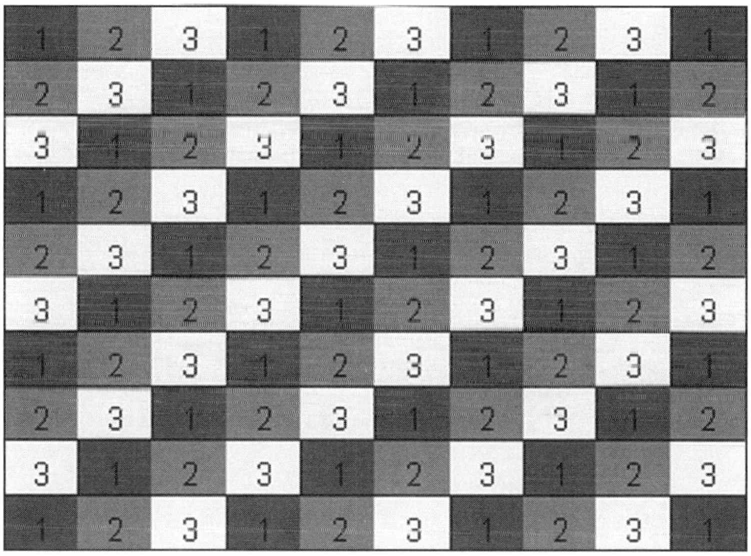

Figure 5.2. A completed Patterns lesson.

Extension

Open the *Patterns & Shapes* template for each student (Figure 5.3). Students begin by repeating a simple color pattern in the first two patterns they complete. They then translate that color pattern to a letter pattern by adding a letter to each cell, A for green, B for yellow, and C for pink. In the third pattern they begin with letters, then add colors. They create their own pattern with letters and colors in the fifth pattern.

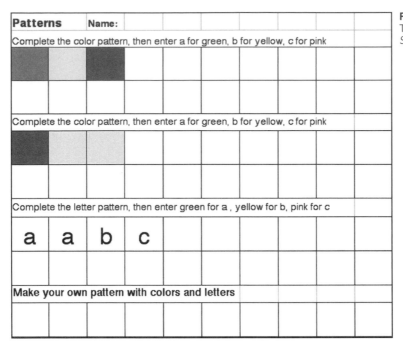

Figure 5.3.
The *Patterns & Shapes* template.

They use the Basic Shapes on the Autoshapes menu to make the shapes pattern (Figure 5.4). It is easiest for them if the teacher demonstrates and helps students tear away this menu and places it on the spreadsheet document where it is easily accessible. To do this, click on the Autoshapes menu, click on Basic Shapes, hold down the mouse and drag the menu by its title bar and position on the document.

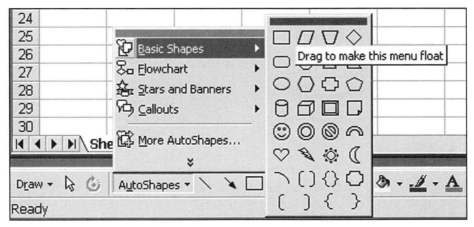

Figure 5.4. The shapes menu can be torn away to float on the page.

Some first graders find it difficult to get the size of the shape right. The trick is to hold down the mouse and drag to the appropriate size. They should not let go of the mouse if the shape is too big, or if the shape is too small, but should drag the mouse until the shape is just right, and then let go. The teacher needs to demonstrate this on computer. Students who find this difficult and frustrating can leave out the shapes examples, and draw them by hand on the hard copy after it is printed out.

To place a shape on the Spreadsheet, click on the shape, move your mouse to where you want to draw it, hold down the mouse and drag. You can resize by clicking on the shape so that it has the handlebars showing, then by holding down the mouse on one of the corners and dragging. To move a shape, click on it to select it, hold down the mouse on the middle of the shape, and drag.

Students repeat the shapes pattern. They then translate that pattern into a numbers pattern, for example 1-2-3-3. The next pattern is complicated, using color and shapes. Students then make their own patterns with shapes.

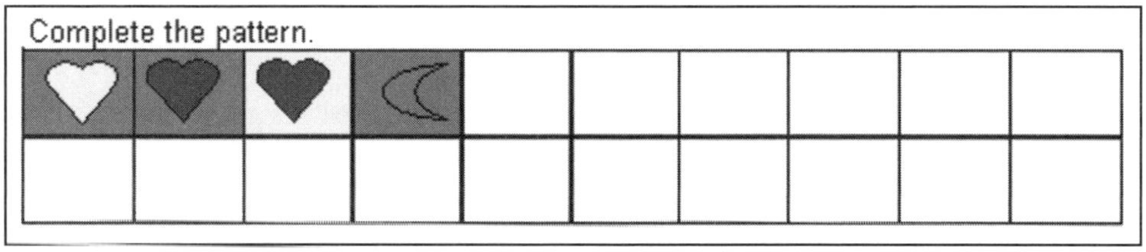

Figure 5.5. An advanced pattern on the *Patterns & Shapes* template.

6. Pets Survey

Lesson Description

Ask your students about their pets at home, and create a class list of the types of pets the students mention. As a class, students record this class information on the *Pets* template and tally it. After learning how to insert a chart, students make their own pictograph using clip art. Engage the class in a discussion of which type of pet is the most popular among classmates, which is second most popular, and which is least popular. A completed spreadsheet lesson is available in the file *Pets Sample* on the CD-ROM.

Higher-Order Thinking Skills	Spreadsheet Skills Practiced	Subject Areas and Standards Addressed
Students understand the reason for doing a survey. They describe the pets they have and the class shares and tallies the information, organizing it on the spreadsheet. They create charts, then analyze the results, and compare to see which pets are most and least popular. They draw conclusions and predict that their findings will be true for a larger population. They then offer personal opinions as to why some pets are more popular than others.	Insert chart Change chart title Insert, move, and resize clip art	NETS•S: 4, 5 Mathematics: 5

Name:				
Pets	**# of Students**	**Tally Marks**		
Gerbil	1	x		
Bunny	1	x		
Dog	11	xxxxxxxxxxx		
Fish	7	xxxxxxx		
Lizard	1	x		
Cat	7	xxxxxxx		
Hermit Crab	2	xx		
Guinea Pig	3	xxx		

Figure 6.1. A line plot tallying the students' pets.

Computer Activity

1. Students participate in making a class list of the types of pets they have at home.

2. Have students open the *Pets* template and type in the pet types under the Pets heading. Going around the class, each student says what type of pet he or she has at home while the entire class inputs tally marks on their spreadsheets.

3. Have students total the tally marks for each pet, and place the total in the # of Students column.

4. After demonstrating how to create a chart from data, have students create a column chart by highlighting the data in columns B and C. In the sample shown in Figure 6.2, students highlight from cell B3 to C11. Then click on the Insert menu and on Chart.

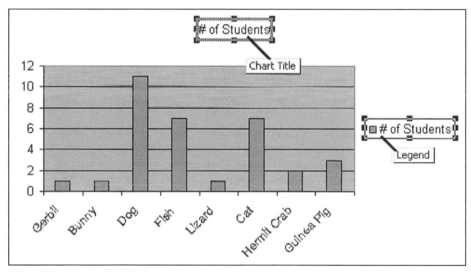

Figure 6.2. A chart showing the student pet data.

5. Have students click on the legend, so that it is selected, and press the Delete key on the keyboard. Students can name their charts by double-clicking on the chart title to get the cursor, backspacing to delete # of Students, and typing in a title such as "Bar Graph of Pets in our Homes."

6. Students can use the chart to make a pictograph. First, have them place the tally marks in vertical columns, which will reflect the number of images they need to place for each animal. From there, they can easily design a pictograph using the *Pets* template. Make sure they label the pets on the pictograph.

7. First-grade students quickly learn how to click on a picture they like, copy it, and paste it in their document. To insert clip art, click on the Insert Clip Art button on the Drawing toolbar. The window shown in Figure 6.3 will open. Type in words to look for pictures. Click on the picture you want, then click on Insert Clip to place it on the spreadsheet.

ClipArt Icon

If you can't find the pictures you need in the Clip Art Library, you can search for them online at Microsoft Office Online's Clip Art and Media Web page by clicking on Clips Online. If you can't or don't wish to go online, have students draw pictures to represent the pets for which clip art isn't available.

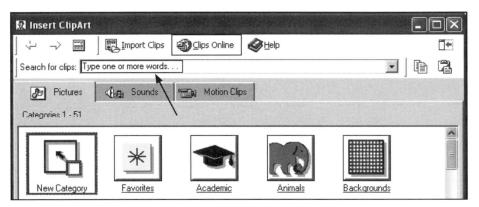

Figure 6.3. You can easily search for clip art in the Clip Art Library.

8. After finishing their charts, the class should discuss how the graphs show which pet is most popular, second most, and least popular. See the file *Pets Sample* on the CD-ROM to view the completed spreadsheet lesson.

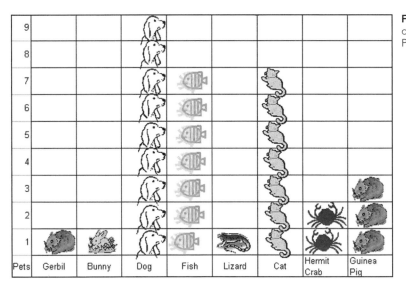

Figure 6.4 A completed Pets Pictograph lesson.

Second-Grade Lessons

7. **Math Problems with 5, 7, and 9** (MATH)

   ▪ Math Problems 1

   ▪ Math Problems 2

8. **Money to Spend** (MATH)

9. **Finding the Rule** (MATH)

10. **Change for a Bill** (MATH)

    ▪ Counting Up to Make Change

11. **Apple Tasting Survey** (MATH)

12. **Bats or Birds?** (LANGUAGE ARTS, SCIENCE)

    ▪ Comparisons

7. Math Problems with 5, 7, and 9

Lesson Description

Students input numbers into grids and use a number line to create math equations that result in answers of 5, 7, and 9. They may practice with these numbers using manipulatives before completing the exercise on the computer.

Higher-Order Thinking Skills	Spreadsheet Skills Practiced	Subject Areas and Standards Addressed
Connect visual representations of numbers and abstract concepts like addition and subtraction Apply what has been learned about addition and subtraction to create new math problems with colors for visual cues Divide a number into two parts, and compare where different numbers lie on the number grid	Enter numbers, plus signs, and equal signs Fill cells with colors or patterns Format borders (Extension)	NETS•S: 3 Mathematics: 1, 3, 6

Math Problems 1

Exercise Description

In this exercise, students can count the squares on the grid and match them with the digits 5, 7, or 9. The grid that they fill with color (or pattern if they do not have access to a color printer) helps students visualize the math problems and understand the meaning of the numbers. The five colored cells in row 5 offers a visual cue to check that the sum is equal to 5. Similar colored cells are provided for 7 and 9.

Computer Activity

1. The teacher opens the *Math Problems 1* template and shows students how the math problems that equal 5 were made. The instructor explains how the number 5 can be made of 5+0, 4+1, 3+2, 2+3, 1+4, and 0+5, and shows how different colors have been used to mark each of these numbers on the grid.

2. The teacher demonstrates how to change the fill color by selecting or highlighting the cell or cells to be changed, then clicking on the arrow next to the Fill Color button and choosing a color. (The cell pattern can be changed if a color printer is not available. Click on the Format menu, click on Cells, and on the Patterns Tab, then click on the arrow next to Pattern to select a pattern.)

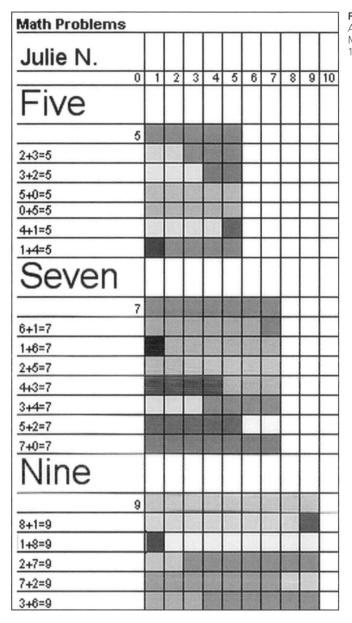

Figure 7.1.
A completed
Math Problems
1 lesson.

3. The teacher shows how to fill the number of cells for each digit in the equation in a color that is different from the color of the cells around it.

4. Students complete the exercise for the number 5, filling cells with color. By looking at the number line at the top of the page (row 5), students can check the math to make sure the equations add up to 5.

5. Students next enter the math equations for 7 and 9. Upon completion, they fill the cells with color.

6. Fast workers can help others to complete the project, and slow workers can print out the sheet with the equations and use colored pencils or crayons to color the squares on the hard copy.

In Figure 7.2, the Fill Color palette has been torn away and moved onto the right side of the document. This simplifies the coloring process. To do this, click on the arrow next to the Fill Color button on the formatting toolbar. When the Fill Color palette window opens, tear it away from the toolbar by holding down the mouse on the title bar and dragging the palette down onto the document.

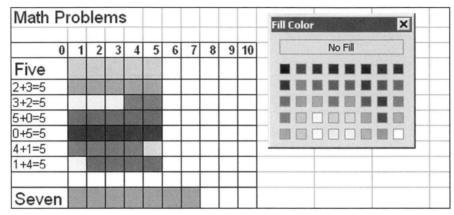

Figure 7.2. Tearing away the Fill Color palette simplifies the lesson.

Extensions

- You may use subtraction as the operation. Students fill the larger number with solid color and then use a pattern to delete the part of the number that is subtracted.

- The following exercise, Math Problems 2, may be used as an extension for students who complete the lesson quickly.

Math Problems 2

Exercise Description

Math Problems 2 offers a different format to teach the same concepts introduced in Math Problems 1 with 5, 7, and 9. In Math Problems 2, vertical, as opposed to horizontal, imagery is used to illustrate addition and subtraction problems. After discussing how the math problems are described with math equations and blocks of color, students make their own math equations to equal the target numbers 5 or 7. Students change the fill color as they count the cells in each number. They put a number in each color block to show the amount the block represents. Students format borders around the blocks.

A demonstration and explanation are necessary as this is a difficult task. The teacher should read through the instructions with students and demonstrate each step.

Students could continue to make math problems in this way on a blank spreadsheet. If larger numbers are used, they may need to change the page orientation to landscape. To do this, click on the File menu, select Page Setup, choose Landscape, and click on OK.

Computer Activity

1. Open the *Math Problems 2* template.

2. Enter math equations that give the answer of 5 in row 11.

3. Highlight the number of cells equaling the first number in your math equation.

4. Change the fill color of those cells.

5. Click on the arrow next to the Borders button on the Formatting toolbar, and choose Outside Borders.

6. Now do the same for the second number.

7. Put a number inside each color block to show the amount the blocks represent.

8. Now do the same for the next math equation.

9. Repeat these steps for equations that give an answer of 7.

10. Under the File menu, select Save and Print.

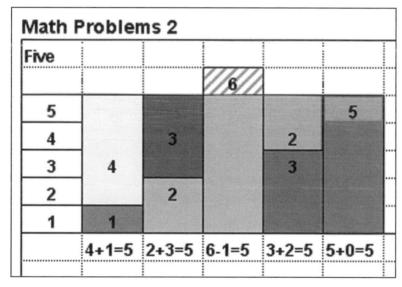

Figure 7.3. A completed Math Problems 2 lesson.

8. Money to Spend

Lesson Description

Students are asked to pretend they won a prize—a $300 gift certificate at a toy store. They need to solve the problem of finding items they would like to buy by spending as close to $300 as possible as they choose toys from a toy catalogue or an online toy store. Students have lots of fun selecting items to put in their spreadsheet. They do not need to do the computations; a formula has been entered on the *Money to Spend* template that calculates a running total of the amount spent. This allows them to focus on the problem-solving aspect of the lesson. Students perceive changes in the total as numbers are entered and develop an understanding of using formulas and functions on a spreadsheet.

When students have more than $200 as their total, they try to estimate how much they need to spend to get to $300. Students who are unable to answer this are encouraged to count by 10s with the help of the teacher. They should begin with the most recent total and work with the teacher to decide what the appropriate price range of the next item should be.

Higher-Order Thinking Skills	Spreadsheet Skills Practiced	Subject Areas and Standards Addressed
Connect what has been learned about addition and subtraction to a real-life situation Estimate and predict what can be bought for a limited amount of money Solve the problem of making the best selections within a budget	Enter numbers and text in cells Format numbers as currency Explore the use of formulas Use the Calculator tool Hide row and column headings	NETS•S: 6 Mathematics: 1, 6, 9

Computer Activity

1. Students open the *Money to Spend* template.

2. Looking at a toy catalogue or an online toy store (such as www.toysrus.com or www.etoys.com) students type objects they would like to buy under Item, in column A.

3. They enter the price of each item under Cost, in column B. They try to spend $300 without going over. Students use the Calculator tool to make estimations to reach the target amount.

4. To format numbers as a currency, students highlight column B, click on the Format menu, then select the Cells tab, Number and Currency. Numbers will automatically be formatted in dollars and cents.

5. Students who finish quickly may like to add clip art.

6. Students save and print.

Extensions

■ Change the total target amount. For example, have younger students buy candies for $10 or older students spend $1,000,000.

■ Students plan a budget for money they receive for an allowance or for doing household chores.

◇	A	B	C
1	Money to spend at the toy store:		
2	Name: Megan J.		
3			
4	You have just won $300.00. You can only spend it if your list adds up to between $299.00 and $301.00.		
5	Item	Cost	
6	Scooter	$59.00	
7	Virtual Reality World Game	$25.00	
8	Cell Phone	$39.99	
9	Electronic v-mail	$17.00	
10	Radio control car	$29.99	
11	Exercise equipment	$29.99	
12	Tekno Robotic Puppy	$49.99	
13	Personal CD Player	$49.99	
14			
15			
16	Total	$ 300.95	
17			
18	Save this list.		
19	Extra Credit:		
20	Click on the Insert menu and select Picture. Insert a picture from Clip Art on your page.		
21	Save and Print.		

Figure 8.1. A completed Money to Spend spreadsheet.

9. Finding the Rule

Lesson Description

Students practice adding, subtracting, and recognizing patterns by completing a sequence of numbers according to a rule. For example, the sequence 2, 4, 6, 8, 10 is given along with the rule "add 2," and students finish the sequence with 12, 14, and 16. Or, students are given a pattern and asked to find the rule. Numbers or rules that are provided on the *Find the Rule* template are formatted in black, and numbers or rules that students enter are formatted in red. This makes checking student work easier. Note that the rules are filled in with words for add and subtract rather than signs, as the computer would automatically enter +5 as 5 in a spreadsheet where cells are formatted as numbers.

Students also create their own rules using the template. They make up a formula to apply the rule, and then use the spreadsheet's computational function to generalize a formula.

Higher-Order Thinking Skills	Spreadsheet Skills Practiced	Subject Areas and Standards Addressed
Analyze number patterns and generalize or complete the pattern	Create and enter formulas	NETS•S: 6
	Show formulas or data	Mathematics: 1, 2, 6
Create original patterns	Extend formulas using the Fill Handle, or Edit, Fill Right	
Invent a formula to apply a rule	Format borders (Extension)	

Computer Activity

1. Students open the *Find the Rule* template.

2. In the first portion, students generalize the rules to complete the sequences of numbers.

3. Students are then required to make up their own rules and sequences of numbers.

4. They use formulas to fill cells according to the rule. Formulas display in the formula bar, but not in the cells. To show the formulas in the cells, click on the View tab, and place a check mark next to Formulas.

Find the Rule

Name:

Fill in the rule and fill in the empty cells according to the rule for the sequence of numbers:

Rule								
Add 2	2	4	6	8	10			

Rule								
Subtract 4	28	24		16		8		0

Rule								
	10	15	20	25	30	35	40	45

Rule								
	3	6						

Rule								
		67	57					

Rule								
Add 6		38						

Rule								
Add 7		20						

Make up your own rule and fill the cells with numbers for that rule:

Rule								

Rule								

Now use formulas to fill the cells all the way to the end of the page.
Look at the example below:

Rule								
Add 5	15	20	25	30	35	40	45	

To see the data in place of formulas, click on the Tools menu and click on Options.
Click on the View tab and remove the check mark next to Formulas.

Figure 9.1. The *Find the Rule* template.

Fill in the rule and fill in the empty cells according to the rule for the sequence of numbers:

Rule								
Add 2	2	4	6	8	10	12	14	16

Rule								
Subtract 4	28	24	20	16	12	8	4	0

Rule								
Add 5	10	15	20	25	30	35	40	45

Rule								
Add 3	3	6	9	12	15	18	21	24

Rule								
Subtract 10	77	67	57	47	37	27	17	7

Rule								
Add 6	32	38	44	50	56	62	68	74

Rule								
Add 7	13	20	27	34	41	48	55	62

Make up your own rule and fill the cells with numbers for that rule:

Rule								
Subtract 5	45	40	35	30	25	20	15	10

Rule								
Add 4	3	7	11	15	19	23	27	31

Figure 9.2. A completed Find the Rule lesson.

5. Students can check their work in the row underneath by typing in the first number, entering a formula in the adjacent cell, and then using the Fill Right function. To fill a formula right, first enter the formula in one cell. Hold down the mouse on the cell containing the formula and drag to the right to highlight where the formula is to be applied. Click on the Edit menu, select Fill, and choose Right. Or, to use the Fill handle, click on the corner of the cell containing the formula, so that the pointer changes to a black cross, and drag to apply the formula to adjacent cells.

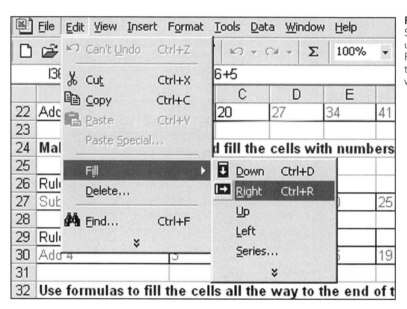

Figure 9.3. Students can use the Fill Right function to check their work.

Extension

Students make up their own rules. They highlight the cells they want borders around, click on the Borders button on the Formatting toolbar, and click on All Borders. They insert numbers to make their pattern, and use formulas to generalize the rule.

10. Change for a Bill

Lesson Description

Prior to using a spreadsheet, students who are learning to make change play shop-keeper and use pretend coins to pay the exact amount. They take turns buying pretend food or toys marked with prices similar to the examples in this lesson.

Students get further practice making change as they complete this lesson. The *Change for a Bill* template allows students to focus on problem solving rather than on making calculations, as the computer does this for them. Imitation coins are used side-by-side with the spreadsheet to help students. The teacher demonstrates how the total changes as numbers are inserted under each column. Students watch the change in total and they estimate which coins to use and how many of each. The class brainstorms how the computer automatically calculates the total, and they answer questions such as "How would you decide how much two quarters makes? So how do you think the computer knows the answer? What happens when you change the number in the Dollar Coin column to 5? Click on each of the cells under Total in column F. What do you notice about the formulas?" Students should observe that the formula is the same for all examples.

Different combinations of coins can be used to reach the target amount. At first, students should try using the fewest possible coins. When they have finished the lesson, they can insert one row under each problem and try to reach the same target amount as contained in the row above using different coin combinations.

Higher-Order Thinking Skills	Spreadsheet Skills Practiced	Subject Areas and Standards Addressed
Apply knowledge about counting money to solve a problem Enter a number for each coin and modify the numbers to reach the target total dollar amount, exploring this in an abstract context Invent original examples	Enter numbers using the number pad Explore the use of formulas Insert rows	NETS•S: 6 Mathematics: 1, 6

Computer Activity

1. Students open the *Change for a Bill* template. They are told that they will use the coins mentioned in row 7 to make the amount in column G.

2. Students are asked to look at the example in row 8 and to change the number in the Dollar Coin column to see what happens to the total. They can try the

same with other numbers in this example. They examine the formula in column F for row 8 and then are led to conclude that the formula is the same for all rows. Students do not need to understand this for the exercise to be useful, as those students who struggle with addition can focus on the problem solving and have the computer make the calculations for them.

3. Using the number pad, students enter numbers in the Dollar Coin, Quarter, Dime, Nickel, and Penny columns to reach the total for each row in the first part of this exercise. The teacher points out how different combinations of coins can be used to reach the target amount. Have students try to use the fewest possible coins.

4. In the second half of the lesson, students create their own examples by first choosing a total and then selecting coins to reach that amount.

5. Students who complete the lesson are encouraged to insert one row under each problem and reach the same target amount as the row above using different coins. They insert rows by clicking on the Calculate menu and selecting Insert.

Counting Up to Make Change

Exercise Description

Students open the *Making Change* template. They use the tool provided to count up but must remember to delete the gray area on the tool to reset it to 0, as they begin a new problem. As they enter a number for the coins under the How Many? heading, the Total and the Total Amount change accordingly. They try to reach the target amount for each problem. $10.00 for the first example, $20.00 for the second, and $5.00 for the third. They then make up their own examples. Formulas have been entered to check their answers. Figure 10.1 shows a sample of the completed exercise.

Students playing the role of cashiers can use this spreadsheet to give the right change when the class plays "Shop for Groceries or Toys."

Extensions

- The class looks at the formulas used in the Making Change lesson, and tries to understand how the counting up tool works. Students try to explain how the cash register at the supermarket "knows" how much change to give to the buyer.

- The class brainstorms other uses for formulas. For instance, a formula could be used to make the calculation if the class was buying an ice cream treat for each student and it cost 75 cents, or if students were going on a field trip that cost $3.00.

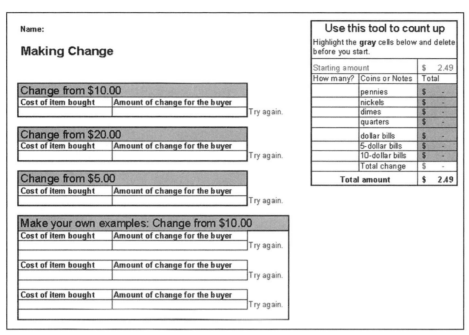

Figure 10.1. A completed lesson using the *Making Change* template.

11. Apple-Tasting Survey

Lesson Description

On Johnny Appleseed Day, September 26, our second-graders have an apple-tasting event where they eat and learn about the different varieties. This year, we conducted a survey to determine the class favorite. Students were given a hard copy of the *Apple-Tasting* template. They distinguished among six varieties of apples in terms of taste and appearance. They used the digital camera to photograph each type of apple before we cut and ate it.

While students tasted the apples, they described what they looked like and tasted like. They shared their reactions and we brainstormed vocabulary—sweet, sour, tart, juicy, flowery, crisp, plain, tasteless, reddish pink, red, green. Students ranked the apples from most to least favorite and entered their findings on the *Apple-Tasting* template (Figure 11.1). We shared our opinions, tallied the class favorites, and determined the class ranking for each apple. We then charted the results using Excel. After completing and printing their charts, students answered the following questions:

- Which is the most popular apple?

- Which is the second most popular apple?

- Which is the least popular apple?

- How many people took the survey?

Higher-Order Thinking Skills	Spreadsheet Skills Practiced	Subject Areas and Standards Addressed
Compare and discriminate, evaluate, rank favorite types of apples Learn new vocabulary words Describe taste and appearance of apples Organize and analyze class results Interpret charts	Insert, resize, and move digital photographs Insert a chart Insert a title for a chart	NETS•S: 4 English Language Arts: 7 Mathematics: 5

Computer Activity

1. Have students take digital images of six apples, then load them on the school server. Store the photos in a folder that students can access. (The teacher can do this step if less time is available for the project.)

2. Open the *Apple-Tasting* template and enter the names of six types of apples.

	Photo	Name of Apple	What It Looks Like	What It Tastes Like	My Ranking	Class Rankings of 1	Class Ranking
Apples We Tasted Name: Megan							
1		Gala	Reddish yellow	Very sweet	1	7	1
2		Red Delicious	Tall and dark red	It was dry, but sweet	6	4	3
3		Yellow Delicious	Yellowish green	Plain, not much flavor	5	0	6
4		Macintosh	It was half red and half green	Sour!	3	1	5
5		Jonathan	Dark red and round	Sour, but good	4	5	2
6		Granny Smith	Lime green	Tart and crisp	2	2	4

Figure 11.1. A completed Apple-Tasting lesson.

3. Click on Insert, Picture, From File, and browse to locate the photographs taken by students. The picture can be resized by dragging on the corner handlebars. Click in the middle of the picture and drag to move it. Place each apple picture inside the cell beside its name.

4. After students taste-test each apple, have them enter their findings on their spreadsheets. They can enter their information directly into the spreadsheet cells if enough computers are available. If not, their findings can be entered on hard copies. When students have finished recording findings for each type of apple, they should rank the apples from most to least favorite, with 1 being most favorite and 6 being least favorite.

5. Students use the *Apple Chart* template to tally the number of apples of each kind that students gave a ranking of 1. Students then enter this information into their *Apple-Tasting* templates so they can see how their own opinion compares to their fellow students'.

6. Students make a chart from their *Apple Chart* templates to illustrate their findings (instructions are on the template).

7. After the chart is created, it can be moved by holding down the mouse inside the chart and dragging it. Students can add the title Apple Survey Results (Figure 11.2). Click on the legend and delete it if you wish.

8. Preview what will print. Click File, Print Preview, then Close to close it.

Extension

Instead of tallying and charting the number of "ranking of 1" scores, try exploring other information, such as least favorite apple or comparing colors of apples to favorites. How would the chart look different if the number 6 represented the favorite apples instead of 1?

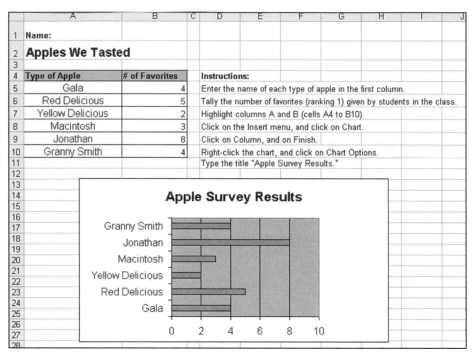

	A	B	C	D	E	F	G	H	I	J
1	Name:									
2	**Apples We Tasted**									
3										
4	**Type of Apple**	**# of Favorites**		Instructions:						
5	Gala	4		Enter the name of each type of apple in the first column.						
6	Red Delicious	5		Tally the number of favorites (ranking 1) given by students in the class.						
7	Yellow Delicious	2		Highlight columns A and B (cells A4 to B10).						
8	Macintosh	3		Click on the Insert menu, and click on Chart.						
9	Jonathan	8		Click on Column, and on Finish.						
10	Granny Smith	4		Right-click the chart, and click on Chart Options.						
11				Type the title "Apple Survey Results."						

Figure 11.2. Use the *Apple Chart* template to tally class totals and create a chart.

12. Bats or Birds?

Lesson Description

Second-grade students read the book *Stellaluna*, by Janell Cannon. As a prelude to writing their own story about a baby animal, use the *Story Sequence* template to examine how the story is organized into parts: a beginning, middle, and end. Look at how events follow in logical, sequential order. Talk about the problem and how it's resolved. Students later use the same template to analyze the structure of a different story, and then to write their own story.

Higher-Order Thinking Skills	Spreadsheet Skills Practiced	Subject Areas and Standards Addressed
Analyze the structure of a story	Enter text in cells	NETS•S: 3
Create an original story	Drag and drop the contents of a cell	English Language Arts: 1, 4, 8
Organize story events in a logical fashion	Edit a spreadsheet and use Undo	Science: C1
Classify animals according to similarities and differences	Resize column width	
	Insert cells	
Apply information learned from a story to distinguish between bats and birds	Insert clip art from the Clip Art Gallery and from Microsoft's Clip Art and Media Web page	
Evaluate how people react to differences in others		

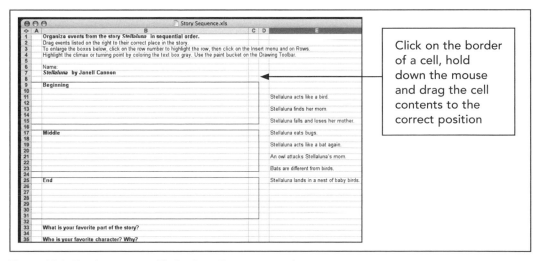

Click on the border of a cell, hold down the mouse and drag the cell contents to the correct position

Figure 12.1. Teachers can modify the *Story Sequence* template.

Computer Activity

1. Modify the *Story Sequence* template by entering events from a story in jumbled order in the cells on the right-hand side. The template starts with *Stellaluna*, but it can be modified to fit any story.

2. Students open your modified *Story Sequence* template. Students put the listed events in the right order, and decide whether each event fits in the beginning, middle, or end of the story. To move the contents of a cell, have students click on the cell border of a sentence they want to move, drag, and let go over the cell where they want to put the text. Make sure students grab the border of the cell. A sample of the completed lesson appears in Figure 12.2.

3. When students are finished organizing the order of events, have them write a sentence about their favorite part of the story or their favorite character.

Note: Students must be told to always move sentences to an empty cell or they will delete the cell contents. When they move the contents of one cell to a new cell address, it replaces what was formerly in that cell. If students don't like where they have placed a sentence, have them drag it to an empty cell on the right until they decide where it should go. If they accidentally delete a sentence, have them choose Undo from the Edit menu to correct their mistake.

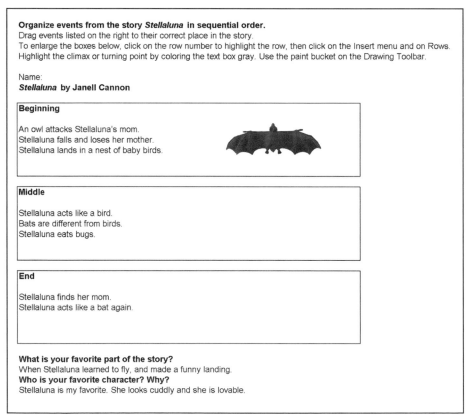

Figure 12.2. A completed story sequence lesson for *Stellaluna*.

Extensions

Instead of providing the events in a list on the right-hand side of the *Story Sequence* template, have students outline on their own a story they have read. They start by entering the main events on the same right-hand column, then dragging and arranging them in the template as they work through what happened when.

Students can use the *Story Sequence* template to write their own story. After brainstorming events on the right, they can drag text into the boxes on the left. They can move their ideas and sentences around until they are happy with the order of events. If students need additional rows, they click on the row heading (a number), click on the Insert menu, then click on Rows. The columns can be expanded in the same way, by clicking on the column heading (a letter), on the Insert menu, then on Columns.

Comparisons

Exercise Description

Students learn about the characteristics of bats when they read *Stellaluna*, and they also learn about the differences between bats and birds. They brainstorm the characteristics of mammals and birds as a class. In pairs, students enter their ideas on the *Bats or Birds* template (Figure 12.3). They clarify their understanding as they sort their ideas. *Stellaluna* also offers an opportunity to explore the notion of prejudice between different groups of people in a non-threatening way, and students have an opportunity to comment on this on the template.

Computer Activity

1. Students open the *Bats or Birds* template. On the template, formatting of borders has already been done and text is centered under each of three headings.

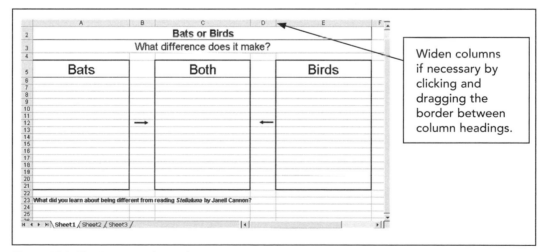

Figure 12.3. The *Bats or Birds* template.

2. Click in the appropriate cell and enter a full sentence. Widen columns if necessary by clicking and dragging the border between column headings.

3. To insert more cells within one of the rectangles, click on a cell, click on the Insert menu, and click on Cell. Click on Shift Cells Down, and on OK.

4. To insert pictures, click on the Insert Clip Art button on the Drawing toolbar. Type in a word to search for a picture, or click on a category to find the picture you want. Click on the picture, and click on Insert Clip on the window that pops up. You can also download clip art from Microsoft's Clip Art and Media Web page. To open this page, click on the Insert Clip Art button then click on the Clips Online button. Add pictures to the selection basket then download and import into your Clip Gallery or Clip Organizer. Save and print a hard copy. Figure I.4 in the Introduction shows a completed Bats or Birds lesson.

Figure 12.4. Appropriate images for the Bats or Birds lesson are available through Microsoft Office Online's Clip Art and Media Web page.

Extension

This template can be used for making other comparisons. The title, headings in the rectangles, and concluding question can easily be changed.

Third-Grade Lessons

13.   **Secret Message: Pledge of Allegiance** (MATH, SOCIAL STUDIES)

14.   **Plot the Points on a Grid** (MATH, SOCIAL STUDIES)

15.   **Creating a Multiplication Table** (MATH)

16.   **Budgeting Money** (MATH)

17.   **Counting Colored Candies** (MATH)

18.   **Classifying Vertebrates** (SCIENCE)

19.   **Brainstorming and Organizing Ideas** (LANGUAGE ARTS)

- Brainstorming from A to Z

- Developing Ideas with Writing Prompts

- Main Ideas and Details

- Brainstorming on a Timeline

- Making Comparisons on a Table

20.   **Designing Place Cards** (MATH, LANGUAGE ARTS)

- Compound Words

13. Secret Message: Pledge of Allegiance

Lesson Description

Students who are learning about locating coordinates on a graph use this spreadsheet lesson to practice this skill. Spreadsheet cells are labeled with "letters across and numbers down," whereas the points on a graph in the "positive, positive quarter" are labeled using number pairs with numbers across and numbers up. A message is scrambled and students use cell coordinates to place the phrases in the correct cells to decode it.

Higher-Order Thinking Skills	Spreadsheet Skills Practiced	Subject Areas and Standards Addressed
Organize and arrange words on the grid, according to cell addresses or points on a quadrant Create a new secret message to be unscrambled (Extension)	Move around the spreadsheet using the arrow, Tab, Enter, Home, and End keys Copy and paste text Delete text Hide row and column headings Format borders Designate specific text to be printed	NETS•S: 1, 3 Mathematics: 3 Social Studies: VIb, d

Computer Activity

1. Students open the *Secret Message* template and enter their names.

2. Using cell coordinates, students copy and paste the phrases in the correct places to read the Pledge of Allegiance. The Copy and Paste features (under the Edit menu) are used in place of Cut and Paste so that if students make a mistake, they can go back and correct it. Students can use the arrow, Tab, Enter, Home, and End keys to move around the spreadsheet.

3. When all text has been correctly placed, students use the Delete key to remove the original phrases.

4. Students remove borders by highlighting the appropriate cells.

5. They hide the column and row headings by clicking on the Tools menu, and on Options, clicking on the View tab, and removing the check mark next to Row & Column headers.

6. Students give the message a new header, "The Pledge of Allegiance."

7. Students save and print the document. They select the print area by high-lighting the cells to be printed and clicking on the File menu and on Print Area, and on Set Print Area.

◇	A	B	C	D	E	F
1	**Secret Message / Coordinates**				Name:	
2						
3						
4						
5						
6						
7						
8						
9						
10						
11	Place the phrases below in the corresponding cells above. You can use Copy and Paste.					
12	C5	for which it stands:				
13	C3	to the flag				
14	A5	and to				
15	A3	"I pledge				
16	C7	for all."				
17	B3	allegiance				
18	B5	the Republic				
19	C6	indivisible,				
20	A7	with liberty				
21	D3	of the				
22	B7	and justice				
23	A4	United States			✛	
24	A6	one nation				
25	B4	of America				
26	B6	under God,				
27						
28	Then, delete these instructions. Give this message a new title.					
29	Save and print.					
30	**Challenge:** Make up your own hidden message on a new spreadsheet for the class to decode.					

Figure 13.1. The *Secret Message* template.

The Pledge of Allegiance   Name: Amanda M.

I pledge	allegiance	to the flag	of the
United States	of America		
and to	the Republic	for which it stands:	
one nation	under God,	indivisible,	
with liberty	and justice	for all.	

Figure 13.2. The completed Secret Message lesson reveals the Pledge of Allegiance.

Extensions

■ Modify the template to include any message you want to reinforce with students—the school mission statement, for example—and then have students decode the message.

■ Students who complete the lesson quickly can make up a message of their own for other students to decode. They print out the template and answer sheet for the teacher to check, and this is then copied for the class to complete.

14. Plot the Points on a Grid

Lesson Description

Students simulate plotting the points of a "positive, positive quadrant" of a graph on a spreadsheet grid. They are reminded that in a number pair, the first number indicates horizontal movement and the second number indicates vertical movement. Students enter the given letters for the cell coordinates on the spreadsheet, print it out, and connect the points on the hard copy to draw the outline of the map of the United States of America. They use the Internet to find the exact distances between cities.

Higher-Order Thinking Skills	Spreadsheet Skills Practiced	Subject Areas and Standards Addressed
Organize and arrange letters of the alphabet on the grid, according to cell addresses or points on a quadrant, to draw an outline Relate the outline to a map of the U.S., and label key cities Use it to compare distances	Move around the spreadsheet using the arrow, Tab, Enter, Home, and End keys Enter and delete text Hide row and column headings	NETS•S: 1, 3, 6 Mathematics: 3 Social Studies: IIIa

Computer Activity

Detailed directions for using the *Plot the Points on a Grid* template are given in the Student Instructions.

Extensions

- Students plot the points to make a map of their state or of a country on a different continent.

- Students make a mystery picture and give instructions to their peers, who then plot the points on a spreadsheet or on graphing paper, join the letters of the "dot-to-dot puzzle," and discover the hidden picture.

- Students calculate the distances between cities in the U.S. and cities in other countries. Maps can be accessed and printed.

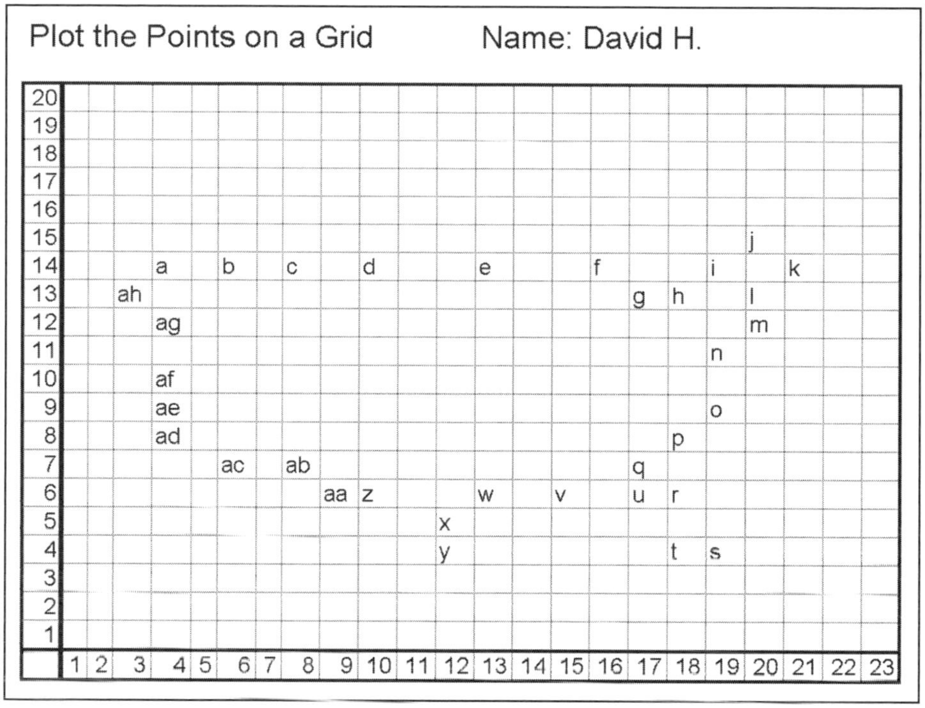

Plot the Points on a Grid   Name: David H.

	1	2	3	4	5	6	7	8	9	10	11	12	13	14	15	16	17	18	19	20	21	22	23
20																							
19																							
18																							
17																							
16																							
15																				j			
14		a	b	c		d			e		f				i		k						
13	ah										g	h			l								
12		ag													m								
11															n								
10		af																					
9		ae													o								
8		ad											p										
7			ac	ab							q												
6				aa	z			w		v	u	r											
5						x																	
4						y					t	s											
3																							
2																							
1																							

Figure 14.1. The completed lesson reveals a map of the United States of America.

<u>Distance</u> between **Seattle, Washington, United States** and **Chicago, Illinois, United States,** as the crow flies:

1737 miles (2795 km) (1509 nautical miles)

Initial heading from Seattle to Chicago:
east (90.4 degrees)
Initial heading from Chicago to Seattle:
west-northwest (295.2 degrees)

Figure 14.2.
A screenshot from the Web site www.indo.com/distance showing the distance between Seattle and Chicago.

Plot the Points on a Grid

Student Instructions

1. Open the *Plot the Points on a Grid* template.

2. To hide row headings and column headings, click on the Tools menu, click on Options, click on the View tab, and remove the check mark next to Row & Column headers.

3. Key in the letter for each of the following number pairs:

a (4, 14)	j (20, 15)	s (19, 4)	aa (9, 6)
b (6, 14)	k (21, 14)	t (18, 4)	ab (8, 7)
c (8, 14)	l (20, 13)	u (17, 6)	ac (6, 7)
d (10, 14)	m (20, 12)	v (15, 6)	ad (4, 8)
e (13, 14)	n (19, 11)	w (13, 6)	ae (4, 9)
f (16, 14)	o (19, 9)	x (12, 5)	af (4, 10)
g (17, 13)	p (18, 8)	y (12, 4)	ag (4, 12)
h (17, 13)	q (17, 7)	z (10, 6)	ah (3, 13)
i (19, 14)	r (18, 6)		

4. Enter your name at the top.

5. Print the lesson with the points plotted.

6. With a pencil, connect the bottom left corner of each of the points from a to b, b to c, and so forth, to ah.

7. Write in a heading for this graphic.

8. Pencil in the following on your printed copy:

    -   Your home town or city
    -   Seattle
    -   New York
    -   Orlando

9. Using the graph you have made, estimate which of the following are closer:

    -   Where you live and Orlando or New York?
    -   Where you live and Chicago or Seattle?

    (Draw a line between the two and measure the distance to get your answer.)

10. Open Internet Explorer or Netscape and check the exact distance between two cities at www.indo.com/distance/. At the Web site you can also access a map showing the two cities.

15. Creating a Multiplication Table

Lesson Description

Students use the grid to make a multiplication table. First they use their knowledge of multiplication to enter data, then they make up formulas to do the calculations.

Higher-Order Thinking Skills	Spreadsheet Skills Practiced	Subject Areas and Standards Addressed
Organize multiplication facts on a grid Analyze how calculations are made, and create a formula to make those calculations	Enter numbers Create and enter formulas Show formulas or data	NETS•S: 1, 3 Mathematics: 1, 2

Computer Activity

1. Students open the *Multiplication Table* template.

2. The numbers 1 through 10 across row 1 and down column A have already been entered.

3. Students multiply intersecting cells and put the answer in the appropriate cell.

◇	A	B	C	D	E	F	G	H	I	J	K	L	M	N	O	P	Q
1	**Multiplication Table**																
2	1. Complete the multiplication table below. Save and Print.																
3	2. Delete all the numbers you just entered.																
4	3. Use formulas so that the computer does the calculations for you.																
5	4. Remember to enter = first, to let the computer know that a formula is coming.																
6	Then click on the cells you want in the formula, rather than type in the cell name.																
7	5. When you have entered all your formulas, click on the Tools menu,																
8	click on Options or Preferences, and add the check mark next to Formulas to show formulas.																
9	6. Print showing formulas.																
10																	
11	Name:																
12																	
13	*	1	2	3	4	5	6	7	8	9	10						
14	1																
15	2																
16	3																
17	4																
18	5																
19	6																
20	7																
21	8																
22	9																
23	10																
24																	

Figure 15.1. The *Multiplication Table* template.

4. They save and print one copy.

5. After printing, they delete all the multiples they have entered (numbers that are not shaded in gray).

6. Students then enter formulas to calculate the multiple of the intersecting cells.

7. They print a copy.

8. To see data rather than formulas, students click on the Tools menu, click on Options, click on the View tab, and remove the check mark next to Formulas. The resulting spreadsheet in which formulas are not shown should be identical to the first copy they printed out.

9. Students can compare their printouts to find any mistakes.

Extensions

- Students look at their printed copy and comment on the number patterns:
    - If you look down the columns, you count by the number that is shaded in gray in row 13. (In column B count by 1s, in column C count by 2s, and so forth.)
    - If you look across the rows, you count by the number that is shaded in gray in column A. (In row 2 count by 1s, in row 3 count by 2s, and so on.)

- Students answer the following question: How would the numbers change in the table…
    - if a 0 were added to the end of each number in row 1 or if the number were multiplied by 10? (Add a 0 to each number on the grid, i.e., multiply it by 10.)
    - if a 0 were added to the end of each number in row 1 and a 0 were added to the end of each number in column A or if the number were multiplied by 100? (Add two zeros to each number on the grid, i.e., multiply it by 100.)

- Students highlight cells on a diagonal from cell 1×1 (B14) to cell 10×10 (K23). These numbers are the squares. This table, or a modification of it, may be useful for teaching squares and square roots to older students.

- The multiplication table is more difficult to complete when the numbers are out of order. Students open the *Mixed-up Multiplication* template and make the calculations, first mentally, then using formulas to check answers, as in the lesson above.

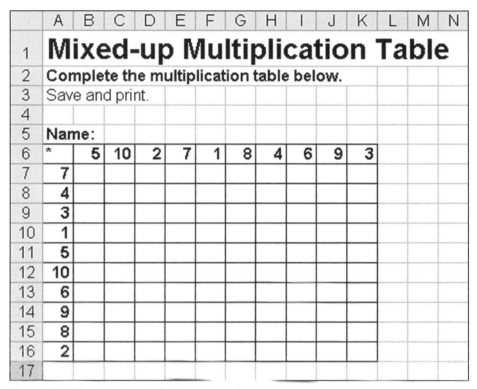

Figure 15.2. The *Mixed-up Multiplication* template.

16. Budgeting Money

Lesson Description

This is a follow-up to the second-grade lesson Money to Spend, where students make a list of toys they would like to buy that totals $300. The Money to Spend lesson needs to be completed before beginning this lesson. In this lesson, they are told that their money is now limited to $50 and that they need to choose which items they will delete to get a total of $50.

The class can brainstorm how they would decide which items to leave on the list and may come up with the idea of sorting the items on their list in descending order according to cost. They would delete items costing more than $50. Next, they delete items they like the least, trying to reach the target total of $50.

The formula for summing the cost of items in column B has already been entered in cell B34 on the *Budgeting Money* template. Depending on the students' level, they may be encouraged to work out or enter the formula themselves. The immediate calculations made by the computer allow the students to focus on the problem of matching the total, and students love to see the total change as they add or delete dollar amounts.

Higher-Order Thinking Skills	Spreadsheet Skills Practiced	Subject Areas and Standards Addressed
Order items according to cost, from most to least expensive Make choices about which items to delete based on a reasoned argument about how many dollars need to be deleted from the total	Sort data in descending order (from largest to smallest) Delete data Create and enter a formula Add clip art	NETS•S: 1, 3, 6 Mathematics: 1, 6, 9

Computer Activity

Detailed directions are provided in the Student Instructions.

1. Students open their Money to Spend lesson, which they had previously saved with a total of $300.

2. The teacher and students read the Student Instructions together.

3. The teacher demonstrates how to sort items in descending order, and then shows how deleting items changes the total.

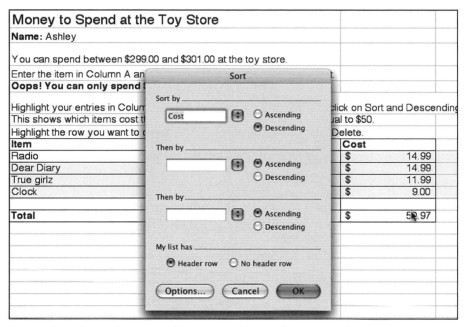

Figure 16.1. After students enter their items and prices, they can sort their lists by cost in descending order.

Extensions

- Change the total target amount. For example, have younger students buy candies for $10.00 or older students spend $1,000,000.

- Students can plan a budget for money they receive for an allowance or for doing household chores.

Budgeting Money

Student Instructions

1. Open your Money to Spend lesson, in which you filled in the items you wanted to buy to total $300.

2. Sort your items from the most expensive to the least expensive.

   - Highlight the items and their prices in columns A and B. Be sure to highlight both columns or the information will get muddled.

   - Click on the Data menu and choose Sort.

   - You want to sort by cost, which is in column B. Click on the arrow next to Sort by, select Cost.

   - Check the button for Descending order (to list the most expensive item first).

   - Click OK.

   - Save your spreadsheet.

3. Delete toys that cost more than $50, by highlighting that row and clicking on the Edit menu, and on Delete.

4. Next, delete items you like the least, aiming to get your total as close as possible to $50.

5. When the empty rows have been deleted, the formula for totaling column B may no longer be valid. The teacher might re-enter the formula for you or might ask you to do it. Here are the instructions for entering a formula to total the numbers in a column.

   - Click on the cell where you want the total to appear and type = (the equal sign). Wherever you click on the spreadsheet afterward becomes part of this formula. The Esc or Backspace key can be used to correct an error.

   - Click on the cell that contains the amount you want to add. Type + (the plus sign) and click on the next cell to add in the total. For example, =B3+B4+B5+B6. (It is not necessary to type in the name of the cell. The computer will put in the coordinate if you click on a cell after typing =).

   - When you press the Enter key, the total amount for the cells in the formula appears in the cell where you entered the formula.

6. Click on the Insert menu and click on Picture, and on Clip Art. Insert a picture on your page.

7. Save as "Spending 50 Dollars" and print.

17. Counting Colored Candies

Lesson Description

Each student receives a small bag of M&M's or other multicolored candies such as Skittles. Students open their bags, sort their candies by color, count the number of each color, and color in a worksheet with the totals.

Students enter their own data in the *M&M's Chart* template and make a pie graph and a bar graph to compare the number of M&M's in each color. They then make a pie graph of class data, and a brief discussion follows in which students interpret the graph.

The author would like to thank Mequon-Thiensville District Technology Department for sharing their ideas on this lesson.

Higher-Order Thinking Skills	Spreadsheet Skills Practiced	Subject Areas and Standards Addressed
Organize candies, sorting according to color Create and interpret charts Make inferences and predictions	Enter data collected Enter a formula Make charts Resize and move charts Modify colors on charts	NETS•S: 1, 3, 4, 5 Mathematics: 5, 9, 10

Computer Activity

1. Students sort their candies by color and count the number of each color.

2. Students receive a hard copy of the *M&M's Bar Graph*. They use colored pencils or crayons to color the correct number of cells to reflect their data.

3. Students open the *M&M's Chart* template.

4. Students enter their data in row 4 to describe their bag of M&M's. They also enter a total in cell G4. The teacher can have them check their total by deleting it and entering a formula so that the computer can make the calculation. The formula is: =SUM(A4:F4).

5. Students highlight cells containing the data they would like to chart, cells A3 through F4. They then click on the Insert menu and choose Chart. They select a column graph by clicking on it, then choose Finish. Students repeat this

procedure to make a pie graph. (Using the bar graph, this is an opportunity to discuss mean, median, and mode with your students.)

6. The two graphs on the page are resized and moved in the same way as any graphic. To resize a chart, click on it to select it, hold down the mouse on one of the corners, and drag. To move a chart, place the cursor in the middle of it, hold down the mouse, and drag. To change the color of slices on a pie chart, click on the color next to the series name in the legend, such as Orange, so that it is surrounded by selection handles. Then click on the arrow next to the Fill Color button on the Formatting Toolbar and click on the color of your choice. You can tear away the Fill Color palette to make changing colors easier.

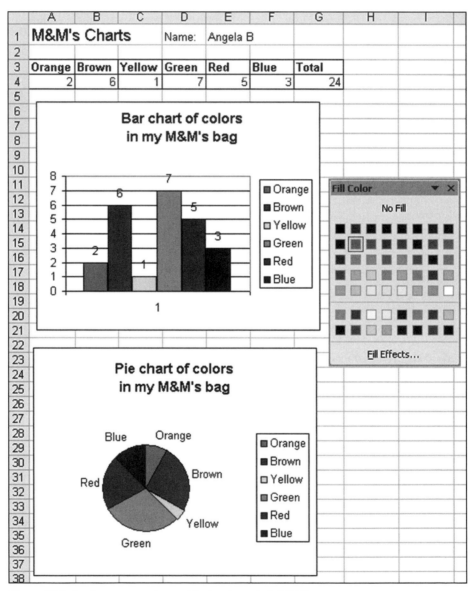

Figure 17.1. Students create charts with data from their M&M's.

7. After completing the computer portion of the lesson, students get into groups of three and answer the following questions:

    A. Why do we draw a graph?

    B. Is it best to compare colors using a pie chart or bar graph?

    C. Why is it better to make the graph on the computer?

    Their answers might include the following:

- The presentation is clear and it is easy to make excellent use of colors.

- It is easy to make a chart and to change it from one type to another.

- It is possible to save and modify the chart by adding data at a later date.

- The data and charts can be shared electronically.

    D. Which color has the most and which color has the least for your own bag?

    E. Compare your graph to your group members' graphs.

    F. Work out your group totals for each color.

8. Leave one bag of candies unopened. Students write down an estimate for the number of candies of each color in that bag. The group with the closest estimate wins the bag to share, but don't open it until after the class data is analyzed.

9. The whole class pools their data to compare the number of each color. Have all the students write their data on a single printed copy of the *M&M's-Class* template next to their names.

10. After all the data is collected, photocopy the spreadsheet so that each student can enter the data for the whole class on his or her own *M&M's Class* template. A formula has been entered on the *M&M's-Class* template under the headings to calculate class totals so that the data can be charted.

11. Students make a pie chart of class data.

12. Have students discuss the lowest number, the highest number, getting a large group total, and comparing colors. Students conclude that we can sum all the scores to get a total and that a pie chart would best show up the comparison of the number of M&M's in each color.

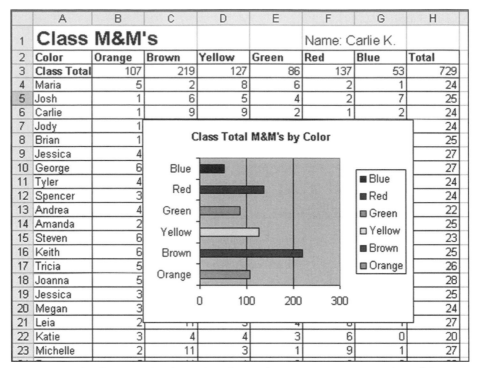

	A	B	C	D	E	F	G	H
1	Class M&M's					Name: Carlie K.		
2	Color	Orange	Brown	Yellow	Green	Red	Blue	Total
3	Class Total	107	219	127	86	137	53	729
4	Maria	5	2	8	6	2	1	24
5	Josh	1	6	5	4	2	7	25
6	Carlie	1	9	9	2	1	2	24
7	Jody	1						24
8	Brian	1						25
9	Jessica	4						27
10	George	6						27
11	Tyler	4						24
12	Spencer	3						24
13	Andrea	4						22
14	Amanda	2						25
15	Steven	6						23
16	Keith	6						25
17	Tricia	5						25
18	Joanna	5						28
19	Jessica	3						25
20	Megan	3						24
21	Leia	2						27
22	Katie	3	4	4	3	6	0	20
23	Michelle	2	11	3	1	9	1	27

Figure 17.2. The class compiles the student data and creates a more accurate chart of the average colors per bag.

Extensions

- Students who complete the lesson quickly can make a bar graph to compare totals and answer the following questions:

  - What is the highest total number of M&M's in a bag?

  - What is the lowest total number of M&M's in a bag?

  - What is the difference between the highest and lowest totals (range)?

- Students survey the class about eye color or favorite sport and make graphs using a spreadsheet or pencil and graph paper.

- Students make a chart to show results in a sports activity at the school, or for a popular state or national team. For instance, students can chart the number of medals won by different countries in the Olympic Games and total them. They can insert clip art images of the flags of each country and place them next to the country names.

18. Classifying Vertebrates

Lesson Description

Students who are studying animals copy and paste text into the *Vertebrates* template, a classification table. Students identify how the animals breathe, whether they are warm- or cold-blooded, and how their body covering differs. They then decide which animals belong in the various categories and copy and paste the pictures into the appropriate cells.

Higher-Order Thinking Skills	Spreadsheet Skills Practiced	Subject Areas and Standards Addressed
Distinguish, classify and compare animal characteristics Illustrate with clip art	Copy and paste text using menu commands or Ctrl, Drag and Drop Extend the contents of a cell using Fill Right Enable text wrapping Copy and paste pictures	NETS•S: 1, 2, 3, 5 Science: C1

Computer Activity

1. Students open the *Vertebrates* template.

2. Students copy and paste the words below the table into the appropriate cells. To copy, click on a cell, pull down the Edit menu, and select Copy (or hold down the Ctrl key and press C). To paste, click on the destination cell, pull down the Edit menu, and choose Paste (or hold down the Ctrl key and press V).

3. When the word is the same in the adjacent cell or cells to the right, encourage students to use Fill Right. They click in the cell containing the word or phrase they want to extend to the right, hold down the mouse, and drag to highlight the cells they want to fill. They then click on the Edit menu and select Fill, then Right (or hold down the Ctrl key and press R).

4. Students will notice that some of the words may be hidden because the cell is too small. To correct this, students change the text wrap. They highlight all the cells in the table, then click on the Format menu, select Cells, and choose the Alignment tab. They then place a check mark next to Wrap text.

5. Students click on each picture to select it, hold down the mouse, and drag it to the appropriate cell describing animals in its group.

6. When the table has been completed, students delete all words under the table, save, and print.

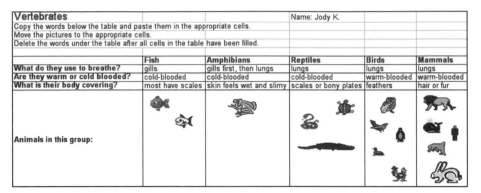

Vertebrates			Name: Jody K.			
Copy the words below the table and paste them in the appropriate cells.						
Move the pictures to the appropriate cells.						
Delete the words under the table after all cells in the table have been filled.						
	Fish	Amphibians	Reptiles	Birds	Mammals	
What do they use to breathe?	gills	gills first, then lungs	lungs	lungs	lungs	
Are they warm or cold blooded?	cold-blooded	cold-blooded	cold-blooded	warm-blooded	warm-blooded	
What is their body covering?	most have scales	skin feels wet and slimy	scales or bony plates	feathers	hair or fur	
Animals in this group:						

Figure 18.1. A completed Vertebrates lesson.

Extensions

- Clip art pictures were inserted on the template to save time for the teacher. Students can be asked to find their own pictures using the Internet. Students need to be told to acknowledge the source of their Internet pictures by copying and pasting the Web address on the document.

- The following Web address has pictures and other useful information: www.seaworld.org/animal-info/animal-bytes/index.htm

- Students can do an online quiz with pictures to identify vertebrates at: www.kidport.com/Grade7/Science/Vertebrates.htm

- Microsoft's Clip Art and Media Web page is a very valuable resource for clip art online. It is necessary to be a licensed Microsoft Office User to use this resource: http://office.microsoft.com/clipart/

- Older students could be given the template without words or pictures underneath and be instructed to find information on the Web sites above to complete the table with the correct text and illustrations.

To copy pictures from the Internet onto a spreadsheet:

1. Open the Web page with a picture you want.

2. Right-click on the picture and select Copy.

3. Minimize the Web browser window (Internet Explorer or Netscape), open the spreadsheet, click where you want to place the picture, right-click, and select Paste.

4. You can minimize the spreadsheet window, return to the browser, find another picture, and repeat.

   Students may find that some pictures will not paste into Excel. Try clicking on Edit, Paste Special.

19. Brainstorming and Organizing Ideas

Lesson Description

This lesson contains four prewriting exercises. They may be completed by individual students, or small groups, or they may be projected for class discussion.

All of the templates can be modified to fit a variety of lessons. Use the *Earth Day ABCs* template to brainstorm ideas from A to Z. Use the *Feeling Words* template to expand vocabulary. With the *Leadership* and *For Sale Poster* templates, students are given writing prompts to explore and organize ideas as a prewriting exercise. The *Brainstorm Timeline* template gives students an outline that helps them structure a persuasive paragraph. Finally, the *Comparison Matrix* template provides a useful tool for comparing and contrasting characteristics and items.

Higher-Order Thinking Skills	Spreadsheet Skills Practiced	Subject Areas and Standards Addressed
Organize and retell ideas that have been shared by students or read on Web pages	Enter text in cells	NETS•S: 6
Evaluate personal ideas and choose one to write about	Format font in the Formula bar	English Language Arts: 5
Read about U.S. presidents and evaluate their leadership qualities	Move between a spreadsheet window and an Internet browser window	Social Studies: VIa, e
Explore a significant event	Resize row height and column width	
Organize and write an original piece based on personal experience	Copy spreadsheet cells using Ctrl, Drag and Drop	
Analyze ideas and classify items according to given criteria		
Identify similarities and differences and make comparisons		

Brainstorming from A to Z

Exercise Description

Students use spreadsheets to capture ideas they have brainstormed, using the letters of the alphabet as a prompt. In both of the examples described below, they use a Web resource to help them generate ideas.

Computer Activity

Earth Day

Students explore ideas to create an Earth Day poster, such as the one in Figure 19.1.

1.   Students open Internet Explorer or Netscape and visit the following Web address to find information about what they can do to help save the Earth (http://pbskids.org/zoom/).

2.   Once they understand what Earth Day is about, students open the *Earth Day ABCs* template. For each letter of the alphabet, students write a sentence that uses that letter about how they can help save the Earth. Students click on the appropriate cells and enter words. A couple of sample sentences are provided on the template.

3.   Students can make the key letter larger or bold so that it stands out. To enlarge the appropriate letter of the alphabet, highlight it in the insertion box and change the size.

4.   Once the sentences have been written, the class discusses which sentences should be included on a class poster promoting Earth Day. They collaborate on creating a final poster in Excel.

Earth Day ABCs	
Name:	
a	Always turn off the lights.
b	Use Both sides of the paper.
c	Always recycle Cans and bottles.
d	Don't leave the water running.
e	The Earth is our home.

Figure 19.1.
A student-created Earth Day poster.

Feeling Words

The class creates an A to Z feelings book, using the *Feeling Words* template to help capture their thoughts (Figure 19.2). They can use an online dictionary (such as www.dictionary.com) or thesaurus (such as www.thesaurus.com) to help them expand their vocabulary. After creating their lists, the students assemble a class alphabet book showing pictures of themselves acting out various feelings.

1.   Each student works with a partner to brainstorm adjectives that describe feelings, beginning with each letter of the alphabet.

2. Students open the *Feeling Words* template, then click on the appropriate cells and enter words.

3. Students open Internet Explorer or Netscape and use the online dictionary or thesaurus to find words starting with a specific letter of the alphabet. (They click on Excel in the taskbar to return to their spreadsheet. Have them click on the Internet window title in the taskbar to reopen the Web page.)

4. Students choose a letter of the alphabet and its associated feeling. Have them pose for a photograph where they act out a feeling beginning with that letter. Students can write a few sentences as clues for a reader to guess the adjective they have acted out, without using the adjective in their description.

5. As a class, the students assemble an alphabet book showing their pictures of feelings.

6. A list of other words starting with that letter can also be put on each alphabet page.

The idea for this lesson came from the Apple iLife Web site where they give details about the project called Feelings from A to Z: (http://ali.apple.com/ali sites/ali/exhibits/1000906/).

◇	A	B	C	D	E	F
1	Feeling Words				http://www.rhymezone.com	
2	a	angry	amazed	afraid	anxious	alive
3	b	bored	better	bad	blessed	bold
4	c	crushed	crazy	cheerful	cozy	curious
5	d	delighted	doubtful	dizzy	determined	disgusted
6	e	excited	eager	evil	envious	easy-going
7	f	frightened	freaky	furious	funny	fit
8	g	grumpy	glad	graceful	good	gentle
9	h	happy	hurt	holy	hopeful	honest
10	i	interested	idle	ill	important	irritated
11	j					

Figure 19.2.
A filled-out *Feeling Words* template.

Developing Ideas with Writing Prompts

Exercise Description

On President's Day, students explore the idea of leadership and generate ideas on the topic. Using the *Leadership* template (Figure 19.3), they brainstorm ideas about leaders they know and clarify the meaning of good leadership, analyzing the leadership qualities these people demonstrate. They explore their own leadership qualities, then share their ideas. Finally, students talk about, then write about U.S. presidents, current or past, and their actions and leadership qualities.

Computer Activity

1. Students open the *Leadership* template (Figure 19.3).

2. After a class brainstorming session, have students fill out the template. They click on the appropriate cell and enter information. The text is wrapped in

the cells, so that the row height should automatically change as information is entered. As cells resize, students may need to move the arrows on the template by clicking on them and dragging.

3. Have students share the information they have entered.

4. Have students write a brief paragraph or essay on their ideas about leadership, using factual information about the current or past U.S. presidents.

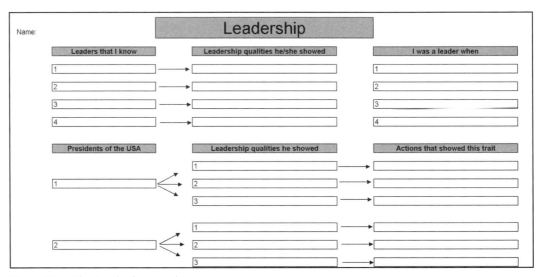

Figure 19.3. The *Leadership* template.

To modify this template for other lessons: To delete a cell, click on it, click on the Edit menu and click on Delete. To add a cell, click on the row header so that the entire row is highlighted, click on the Insert menu, and on Row. Click on the cell to highlight it, format the border by clicking on the Borders button on the Formatting toolbar. To wrap the text in a cell, click on the cell to highlight it, click on the Format menu, click on Cell, and on the Alignment tab. Add a check mark next to Wrap text.

Main Ideas and Details

Exercise Description

Students think carefully about what they will write in a persuasive paragraph, planning and organizing their ideas in response to writing prompts. They begin with main ideas, and expand to include details.

Computer Activity

1. Students open the *For Sale Poster* template.

2. They enter their ideas in the cells with writing prompts. Cell borders have already been formatted, and cells have been resized.

3. Students modify the template as they fill cells with color, add arrows, insert or delete rows and columns, and insert graphics. They can also use drag and drop to move cells on the grid. Alignment is formatted so that text will wrap in a cell, after the student types it in and presses Enter. To expand the size of a cell, students can resize the appropriate column or row by dragging on the line between row headers or column headers (Figure 19.4).

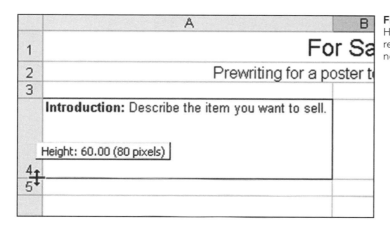

Figure 19.4.
Have students resize rows if necessary.

Brainstorming on a Timeline

Exercise Description

Students brainstorm ideas inspired by a timeline, then choose an idea to write about. They use the prompts of who, what, why, when, where, and how to expand their ideas, which they then drag to organize. They then print the spreadsheet and use it to guide them as they write a final paragraph.

Computer Activity

1. Have students open the *Brainstorm Timeline* template.

2. Have them enter the years they were a specific age above the timeline, and significant first-time events beneath the line. The text has been wrapped in the cells under the timeline. If students need to expand the row height, have them drag on the line between row headers (Figure 19.4).

3. After answering the questions, students should move them into the desired order. Have them click on a cell border to select it so that the cursor changes to a cross, then drag the cell contents to the destination cell on the left. A sample of the completed lesson appears in the Introduction (Figure I.2).

Making Comparisons on a Table

Exercise Description

Students can learn about comparing and contrasting a variety of things using the *Comparison Matrix* template (Figure 19.5). The template is set up with tables to compare the characteristics of animals for a science lesson, and to define nouns for a language arts lesson. A third table is left blank for the student to compare items of his or her choice.

Name:

Animals

Comparison Matrix	Characteristics					
Items to Compare	sleeps	breathes	eats	walks	swims	flies
dolphin						
eagle						
tree						
goldfish						
frog						
elephant						

Nouns

Comparison Matrix	Characteristics			
Items to Compare	person	place	thing	idea
boy				
city				
book				
love				
dog				
classroom				
friendship				
student				

Title

Comparison Matrix	Characteristics			
Items to Compare				

Figure 19.5.
The Comparison Matrix template.

Examples to offer for discussion could include characteristics of various pastimes, such as loud, quiet, fast, slow, educational, and social. Items to compare might be electronic games, board games, sports, or reading. Characteristics of a good sportsmanship could be examined, such as ball sense, running fast, being competitive, being a good team player, or following the rules. In this case, the items to compare might be different sports or famous players. Foods could be classified into various types—grains, vegetables, fruits, milk, meat and beans, and extras (sugar and fats), and students could be referred to the new Food Pyramid (www.mypyramid.gov). Students could insert what they ate yesterday in the Items to Compare column. Or, items to compare could be answers to questions such as, "What I have," "What I want," and "What I need."

In Figure 19.6, the *Comparison Matrix* template was modified for comparing colors used in flags and their symbolic meaning. Students copied and pasted pictures of flags, and identified the colors used on the comparison table. They then read about the symbolic use of colors in flags at the Enchanted Learning Web site (www.enchantedlearning.com/geography/flags/colors.shtml). This modified template, *Colors of Flags*, is available on the CD-ROM.

Pictures of flags are available at Microsoft's Clip Art and Media Web page, which can be accessed by clicking on the Clip Art button, and then clicking the Clips Online button. A good time to do this may be during the Olympic Games. Students also copy and paste the Olympic flag, then design their own flag, selecting colors to use for their symbolic meaning.

Paste a picture of the flag of 10 countries participating in the Olympic games.
Choose two from each of the regions symbolized in the Olympic flag.

Flag	Country	Red	White	Blue	Yellow	Green	Black
	USA	x	x	x			
	Canada	x	x				
	France	x	x	x			
	United Kingdom	x	x	x			
	Zambia	x			x	x	x
	Egypt	x			x		x
	Australia	x	x	x	x		
	New Zealand	x	x	x			
	China	x			x		
	Japan	x	x				
What these colors represent:		Courage, hardiness, revolution	Peace, Purity, Innocence	Freedom, Justice, Peace, Patriotism	Sun, Wealth, Justice	Earth, fertility, agriculture, Moslem religion	Determination, ethnic heritage, defeating enemies

Design a new flag to represent your school or your family
What colors, shapes and symbols will you use? Why?

Figure 19.6. A modification of the *Comparison Matrix* template using national flags.

Computer Activity

1. Students open the *Comparison Matrix* template (Figure 19.5) and enter text in the formatted cells. They may insert an X to select a cell, or may enter words to give details. They resize column width and row height, and delete or insert rows as needed.

2. In the first table, students compare animal characteristics.

3. In the second, they identify the characteristics of nouns, deciding whether they name a person, place, thing, or idea.

4. They give the third table a name, and choose items to compare according to characteristics they specify.

20. Designing Place Cards

Lesson Description

The lesson begins with a class discussion about how different people celebrate holidays, often by gathering for a meal, and how they may decorate to make a festive atmosphere. Students make personalized place cards for a family dinner for a special occasion like Thanksgiving, Christmas, Kwanzaa, Chanukah, or New Year. They view one printed sample place card where the words have not been flipped, and they are upside down when the card is folded over. They brainstorm how this problem could be solved, trying it with pencil and paper first. It is easier to flip WordArt than graphics in Excel, and the teacher, or a student who knows how, demonstrates how to do this on computer.

A second sample is printed out with the words that have been flipped, so that both the picture and the words are upright when folded over. Place cards may be printed on colored paper, for example orange for Thanksgiving, and then printed on a black and white only printer. Students type in the names of the people who will be seated at the table, paying careful attention to the correct spelling of names, checking them at home before they do the lesson. They try to center the word on the card. They then select clip art to decorate each card.

After printing, students cut along the lines and fold on the dotted line between the name and the picture, so that the words are right-side up when the cards is folded and standing. Students at our school enjoyed making these for their families, and one parent even returned after school and asked if her son could make more so that everyone at her Thanksgiving dinner would have a place card.

Higher-Order Thinking Skills	Spreadsheet Skills Practiced	Subject Areas and Standards Addressed
Solve a symmetry problem, making and printing a card that will be folded over, ensuring the words and the picture remain upright on both sides Design a product that may be used for a family celebration Use visual cues to try to comprehend other student's words Analyze words and separate a whole word into its parts	Insert and resize clip art Modify, move, and format WordArt Advanced users insert WordArt, and flip it vertically and horizontally	NETS•S: 3 English Language Arts: 6 Mathematics: 3

Computer Activity

1. Have students open the *Place Cards* template (Figure 20.1).

Figure 20.1.
On the *Place Cards* template, words have been flipped vertically and horizontally so that they will be right-side up when the card is folded over.

2. Have them double-click on the word "Greetings" on the template so that it can be edited. If students do not have the WordArt selected, their typing will be entered in the cell and will sit behind the WordArt. If this happens, press enter, click on the cell and press delete, then double-click the WordArt and try again.

3. Once selected, the Edit WordArt Text window opens (Figure 20.2) and students can replace the text with their own message.

Figure 20.2.
The Edit WordArt Text window.

4. Students repeat the process with "Name," entering the name of a person who will be seated at the table for this special occasion. They can do the same for the rest of the place cards.

While typing in the new text, students can modify the WordArt in several ways.

- WordArt may be resized, in the same way that graphics are resized, by clicking on it so that the handlebars show, and dragging from corner to corner. It is also moved like a piece of clip art.

- Choose a different style of WordArt by clicking on the WordArt to select it, and clicking on the WordArt Gallery button on the WordArt toolbar. (If the WordArt toolbar is not showing, click on the View menu, and click on Toolbars, and add a check mark next to WordArt.)

- To change the color of the fill and lines, click on the Format WordArt button.

- To change the shape of the WordArt, click on the WordArt Shape button.

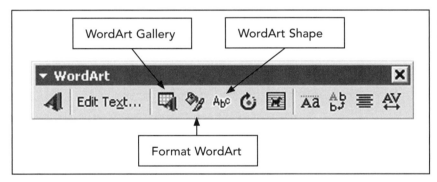

Figure 20.3.
The WordArt toolbar.

5. Have students click on the Insert menu, then the Clip Art button to insert an appropriate picture on the back of the place card. To duplicate it, students simply select it, hold down the Ctrl key, and press the letter D. They can then move the duplicate picture to another card.

6. When all the pictures have been inserted and all the WordArt edited, students click on the File menu, then Print Preview to check their work. Then have them print a hard copy. They can change the names and repeat the steps above to make more place cards.

Extension

Students who would like a challenge can delete all WordArt from the template, and insert their own WordArt. The words need to be flipped vertically and reversed. To do this, they click on Draw on the Drawing menu and select the WordArt button, which opens the WordArt window. After entering their text, they can click on Rotate or Flip, and choose Flip Vertical. An example may be printed out, and students will see that they also need to flip the words horizontally.

To do so, have students click on it to select it, click on the Draw menu, and click on Rotate or Flip, and on Flip Vertical, then repeat this and click on Flip Horizontal.

Compound Words

Exercise Description

Students and the teacher brainstorm a list of compound nouns, or other compound words. They discuss how a compound word consists of two words joined together to make one. A list has been included in the template *Compound Words*, but the teacher may choose to delete this before sharing the file with students.

Computer Activity

1. Have students open the *Compound Words* template (Figure 20.4). They use clip art to represent the two separate words, putting the pictures on one side of the folded card, and the word on the other. When they have printed, cut out and folded the cards, they hide the words from a partner and try to guess each other's words by looking at the pictures.

2. Students double-click on each WordArt word, type in a compound word, and click on OK.

3. Students insert clip art.

4. The print area has been set to include only the words and pictures—the instructions will not print. Have students cut out the cards along the lines, fold along the dotted lines, then use the cards to guess each other's words.

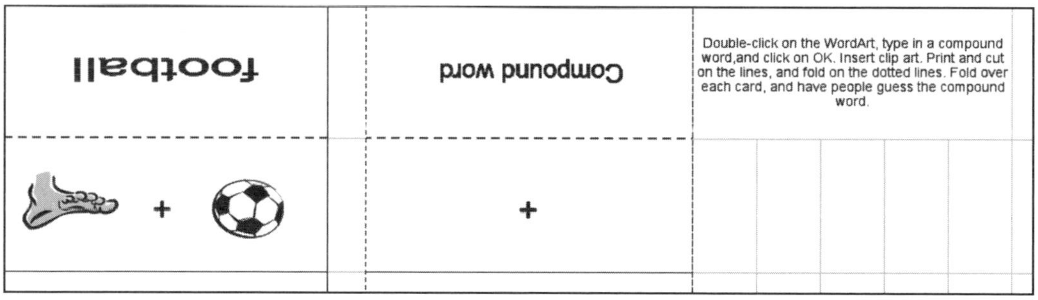

Figure 20.4. The *Compound Words* template.

Fourth-Grade Lessons

21. **Word Search** (LANGUAGE ARTS)

22. **Magic Square** (MATH)

23. **My Measurements** (MATH)

24. **Formulas for Converters** (MATH, SCIENCE)

25. **Visualizing Fractions** (MATH)

- Equivalent Fractions

- Colored Fractions

- Fractions: Greater Than or Less Than?

26. **Music Survey** (MATH, MUSIC)

27. **States and Capitals** (SOCIAL STUDIES)

21. Word Search

Lesson Description

In this exercise, students practice spelling and recognizing vocabulary words by making a word search using a spreadsheet grid. You can type into the *Word Search* template a list of spelling or vocabulary words for your students to use. Or, students can generate their own list of words relating to a topic of study. After students enter their words on the grid, they color them red to create an answer key, fill all other cells with misleading letters in black, and save and print this model answer sheet. They then change all the letters to black, print the word search, and exchange it with a partner to solve. Finally, they check their partner's answers against their answer sheet.

Higher-Order Thinking Skills	Spreadsheet Skills Practiced	Subject Areas and Standards Addressed
Create a word search for other students to solve Generate a word list on a given topic, to review vocabulary and spelling	Enter text in a cell Change the color of text Move around the spreadsheet using the arrow, Tab, and Enter keys Save, print, and modify a document	NETS•S: 1, 3 English Language Arts: 3

Computer Activity

1. Students open the *Word Search* template (Figure 21.1).

2. They enter a list of words below the heading Word List. Once they've typed in enough words, they place the words on the grid. On the grid, words can be entered left to right, right to left, top to bottom, bottom to top, or diagonally. Students move around the spreadsheet using the arrow, Tab, and Enter keys.

3. When students have entered all their words on the grid, they change the color of the words to red, so that they have an answer key. Have students highlight the cells, click on the arrow next to the Font Color button on the Formatting toolbar, and select red. (If the Formatting toolbar isn't showing, students can click on the View menu and on Toolbars, then check Formatting.)

4. After coloring the real words, students finish filling out the grid by entering random and misleading letters (words spelled almost the same as the target words) in the blank cells. These letters automatically appear in black. Students save this as "Answer Sheet" and print it out.

Figure 21.1.
The *Word Search* template.

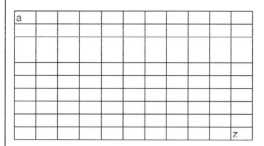

Word Search   Name:

Make your own word search puzzle!
1. **List the words you will use under Word List below.**
2. **Fill in the letters of those words on the grid. Words can go left to right, right to left, top to bottom, bottom to top, or diagonal.**
3. **Create an answer key by changing the words to red.**
4. **Save the puzzle as Answer Key.**
5. **Fill any empty square with random letters, and make all letters black.**
6. **Delete these instructions and type new instructions for the person who will solve your puzzle.**
7. **Save your word search puzzle as Word Search 2.**

WORD LIST:

5. To finish the puzzle, students need to highlight all of the text and change it to black.

6. This document is saved as "Word Search 2." It is printed and given as a challenge to a partner, who circles the words.

7. After their partner has completed the puzzle, each student checks the answers using the answer sheet.

Extensions

- Teachers generate additional word searches for students by using the *Word Search* template.

- This lesson is used for reviewing vocabulary, spelling words, definitions, synonyms, and antonyms in language arts, foreign language, social studies, and science.

22. Magic Square

Lesson Description

Students practice addition by making magic squares using pencil and paper. On a magic square, the sum of each row, the sum of each column, and the sum of each diagonal must all be equal. Figure 22.1 shows a 3 x 3 magic square in which all the totals add up to 15.

Two templates are provided for this lesson. The *Magic Square with Formulas* template includes formulas in the totals cells, while students can enter their own formulas in the *Magic Square* template. On both templates, the totals cells are colored yellow. As students solve the problems using the *Magic Square with Formulas*, have them discuss how the spreadsheet calculator and formulas make solving the magic square easier to do on the computer. The computer does all the calculations and helps students avoid addition mistakes, so students can concentrate on problem solving. Then have them use the *Magic Square* template and try to create their own formulas.

Higher-Order Thinking Skills	Spreadsheet Skills Practiced	Subject Areas and Standards Addressed
Invent algebraic formulas to calculate totals, using mathematical models in an abstract context Solve the problem of making all totals equal Examine whether a formula can be generalized Modify a number and explore how this impacts other numbers, answering the question "What if …?"	Enter numbers Create and enter formulas Show formulas or data in the cells Format borders and column widths (Extension)	NETS•S: 6 Mathematics: 1, 2

Computer Activity

1. Have students open the *Magic Square with Formulas* template and demonstrate how to create a 3 x 3 magic square that totals 15 in all directions.

2. Let students experiment with both the 3 x 3 and 4 x 4 magic squares, encouraging them to change numbers on the magic square to see what happens to the totals. Discuss how a formula is totaling the numbers entered, and what that formula might be.

3. Students open the *Magic Square* template, which has no formulas.

	A	B	C	D	E	F
1	**Magic Square**				Name: Jake L.	
2						
3	6	4	5	15		
4	4	5	6	15		
5	5	6	4	15		
6	15	15	15	15		
7						
8	1	2	3	4	10	
9	4	3	2	1	10	
10	2	1	4	3	10	
11	3	4	1	2	10	
12	10	10	10	10	10	

Figure 22.1.
A completed Magic Square lesson.

4. Working in pairs, students enter their own formulas in the colored cells to make a 3 x 3 and a 4 x 4 magic square. They enter = (an equal sign) to let the computer know that a formula is being entered—after that, if they click in a cell, the cell address will become part of the formula. By entering cell addresses instead of numbers, they can change the target totals and use the same formulas for another magic square. To get out of a formula that has gone wrong, students must press the Escape key.

5. When all the formulas have been entered, students need to fill the squares with numbers that add up to the same total at the end of each row, column, and diagonal. If students struggle with solving the 4 x 4 square, they should be encouraged to solve a second 3 x 3 square.

6. When students have completed two or more magic squares, they save and print two copies: one showing the numbers, and one showing the formulas. To show formulas, click on the Tools menu, select Options, click on the View tab, and add a check mark next to Formulas. Remove the check mark next to Formulas to show data in cells.

Extensions

- Students answer the following "What if ... " questions once they have entered the formulas and numbers for their 3 x 3 magic square (e.g., for totals of 15).

    1. What would happen to the totals if you changed one number in each row by adding 2 to it? Your changes must not be in the same column. (Your totals would now be 17.)

    2. What would happen to the totals if you changed one number in each row by adding 2 and one number in each column by adding 3? (Your totals would be 20.)

- Students with advanced computer skills may create their own magic squares.

1. Have students open a blank spreadsheet document.

2. Students can resize columns by clicking on the Format menu and selecting Column Width.

3. Students can format borders by highlighting the desired spreadsheet cells, clicking on the arrow next to the Borders button on the Formatting toolbar, and choosing the type of border they want.

4. Students enter formulas and numbers following the Computer Activity instructions.

	A	B	C	D	E
1	**Magic Square**				Name: Jake L.
2					
3	8	4	5	=A3+B3+C3	
4	4	5	6	=A4+B4+C4	
5	5	6	4	=A5+B5+C5	
6	=A3+A4+A5	=B3+B4+B5	=C3+C4+C5	=A3+B4+C5	
7					
8	1	2	3	4	=A8+B8+C8+D8
9	4	3	2	1	=A9+B9+C9+D9
10	2	1	4	3	=A10+B10+C10+D10
11	3	4	1	2	=A11+B11+C11+D11
12	=A8+A9+A10+A11	=B8+B9+B10+B11	=C8+C9+C10+C11	=D8+D9+D10+D11	=A8+B9+C10+D11

Figure 22.2. A completed Magic Square lesson with the formulas showing.

23. My Measurements

Lesson Description

Students measure their height in inches using a yardstick or tape measure. They convert this measurement into feet and inches. Students also measure their arm span (from the fingertips of one hand, across the back, to the fingertips of the other hand), the length of the arm from elbow to shoulder, and the length of the leg from hip to knee, in both inches and feet and inches. They learn about the ratio of a human's height to arm span, and that the femur is the longest bone in the human body.

At the beginning of the year, students record their measurements on the worksheet with a pencil and then make a spreadsheet to record the data. At the end of the year they re-measure and add the data to the spreadsheet. They chart all the data to evaluate growth during the year.

The author would like to thank Mequon-Thiensville District Technology Department for sharing their ideas on this lesson.

Higher-Order Thinking Skills	Spreadsheet Skills Practiced	Subject Areas and Standards Addressed
Compare measurements at the beginning and end of the school year	Enter data collected	NETS•S: 6
	Make charts	Mathematics: 4, 5
Compare students' own measurements with those of an adult, and predict the time it will take to grow to a certain height	Change the title of charts	Science: C1
Convert measurements—feet to inches and inches to feet		

Computer Activity

1. Students discuss their measurements as they answer the questions on the *My Measurements Worksheet* (Figure 23.1). For instance, the femur is the longest bone in the body, and arm span and height measure the same.

2. They open the *My Measurements* template and follow instructions.

3. Students enter their measurements from the worksheet for the first date in inches.

4. To chart their first set of measurements, students click in cell B7 labeled "Height," drag to highlight the data they want to include in the chart, click on the Insert menu, and select Chart.

My Measurements

Name:

At the Beginning of the Year:

Enter your measurements in the table below in inches:

Date	Height	Arm Span	Knee to Ankle	Shoulder Width
1-Oct	54	52	25	12
1-Mar	58	55	26	13

1. Highlight from cell A6 to E7, click on the Insert menu, and select Chart.
2. Underneath Chart Type, click on Bar.
3. Click Next, select Rows, click Next again, and type in My Measurements in the title. Click Finish.
4. Save your spreadsheet. We will enter your measurements again in 6 months.

At the End of the Year:
1. Highlight from cell A7 to E8 (both rows), click on the Insert menu, and select Chart.
2. Click Next, select Rows, then click Next again and type in "My Growth Chart" in the title.
3. Click on Finish.

Figure 23.1. Students fill out the *My Measurements Worksheet.*

5. Students follow instructions on the template to remove the word "Series."

6. Students save the file.

7. After measuring themselves on the second date, students enter the second row of measurements and repeat steps to make a chart of all cells in the table. They should modify the second chart according to the instructions.

8. Students double-click on the title of the second chart and type in a new heading, "My Growth Chart."

9. Students may save and print the document.

	A	B	C	D	E	F
1	**My Measurements**					
2	Name:					
3	At the Beginning of the Year:					
4	Enter your measurements in the table below in inches:					
5						
6	Date	Height	Arm Span	Knee to Ankle	Shoulder Width	
7	1-Oct	54	52	25	12	
8	1-Mar	58	55	26	13	
9						
10	1. Highlight from cell A6 to E7, click on the Insert menu, and select Chart.					
11	2. Underneath Chart Type, click on Bar.					
12	3. Click Next, select Rows, click Next again, and type in My Measurements in the title. Click Finish.					
13	4. Save your spreadsheet. We will enter your measurements again in 6 months.					
14	At the End of the Year:					
15	1. Highlight from cell A7 to E8 (both rows), click on the Insert menu, and select Chart.					
16	2. Click Next, select Rows, then click Next again and type in "My Growth Chart" in the title.					
17	3. Click on Finish.					
18						

Figure 23.2. The *My Measurements* template.

Extension

At the end of the year, students may calculate how much they've grown and discuss human growth. They may ask their parents or guardians to measure their height. Based on how much they grew in nine months, they predict how long it will take until they are as tall as their parent or guardian.

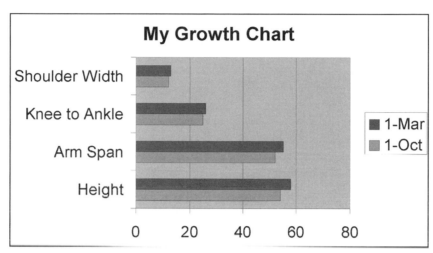

Figure 23.3. A student's completed My Growth Chart.

24. Formulas for Converters

Lesson Description

Converters show how useful formulas can be and help illustrate how they work. Using the *Converters* template, students explore how, as one number changes, the formula calculates a new conversion. Students then brainstorm how the formula in cell C10, which converts from feet and inches to inches, is made. They discuss how to make formulas to convert from miles to feet, inches to feet to yards, tons to pounds, and pounds to ounces. They enter these formulas in the appropriate cells. This lesson works as a nice extension to lesson 23, My Measurements. Students who complete that lesson can enter their measurements on the *Converters* template.

Higher-Order Thinking Skills	Spreadsheet Skills Practiced	Subject Areas and Standards Addressed
Analyze how the computer makes conversions	Enter data collected	NETS•S: 3
Invent algebraic formulas to make conversions	Create and enter formulas	Mathematics: 1, 2, 4
Make connections between different units of measure	Format borders	

Computer Activity

1. Students open the *Converters* template (Figure 24.1) and follow instructions.

2. Students enter their height in inches in cell A6 and then in feet and inches in cells A10 and B10. They notice how the numbers in some other cells change. The class brainstorms how the computer did this. The teacher may lead a discussion about how the computer converts miles to feet, inches to feet, feet to yards, and so forth.

3. Next, students convert miles to feet (there are 5,280 feet in a mile). They enter the number 1 in cell B21. Then they click in cell B22, enter the formula =B21*5280, and press Enter. They will note that the number of feet change when they change the number of miles in cell B21. The correct formulas appear in the Converters Sample file (Figure 24.2).

4. Students complete the other converters on the template. Not all fourth-grade students may be able to work out the formulas for themselves. The teacher can write up the formulas for students to enter in cells.

5. Students may create converters of their own, using measurements of time, for instance. They can format borders for their converters by highlighting cells, clicking on the arrow next to the Borders button on the Formatting toolbar, and making a selection.

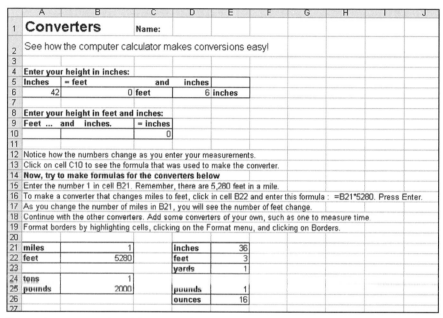

Figure 24.1. A completed Converters lesson.

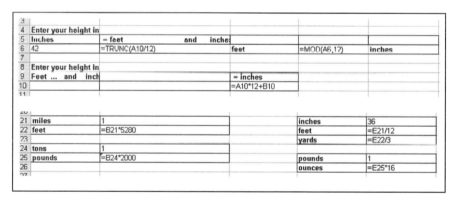

Figure 24.2. The correct formulas for the Converters lesson.

Extensions

Older or advanced students make converters to convert from U.S. customary units of measurement to metric units of measurement. Currency converters can also be made.

25. Visualizing Fractions

Lesson Description

Students have problems understanding the concept of fractions. Try bringing a pizza, apple, cake, or bag of candies into class and have them decide what would be the fairest way to divide it among themselves. It might be useful to have more than one example to show equivalence and address questions such as "Is half an apple equal to half a pizza, or half a bag of M&M's?"

The three exercises that follow are designed to help students visualize fractions as part of a whole. In the first exercise, Equivalent Fractions, students notice that the size of one half changes depending on the size of the whole, and the way they decide what makes a half depends on how many pieces make up the whole. In the second exercise, Colored Fractions, they see that a whole can be divided into different fractions. Although both of these exercises could be completed without the use of a computer if the lessons were printed out and students used colored pencils to do the shading, they can be done quickly and easily on a computer. It isn't necessary to print these two exercises.

The spreadsheet lends itself well to the third exercise, Fractions: Greater Than Or Less Than?, as students format borders to divide a whole made of 40 cells into different-sized segments. They determine the size of each part, then format borders around one segment and use the Copy and Paste features to fill all 40 cells. If they have made a mistake in their calculations they will see that the whole bar cannot be filled with equal-sized pieces.

Before students begin these lessons, set up the Excel workspace (or have your students do it). Make sure the Fill Color and Pattern buttons are showing on the toolbar (click on Tools, Customize, Format, and drag the desired button to the toolbar). Also, tear away the Fill Color and Pattern palettes so that they float on the document (click on the Pattern arrow, and drag the window free). Detailed instructions for both of these are available in "Quick Reference Guide for Using Excel" at the beginning of this book.

Higher-Order Thinking Skills	Spreadsheet Skills Practiced	Subject Areas and Standards Addressed
Connect visual representations and the abstract concept of fractions Compare and discriminate between fractions Invent new fractions, and find a new way to show these fractions	Fill cells with color or pattern Format borders	NETS•S: 3 Mathematics: 1, 3

Equivalent Fractions

Exercise Description

Students learn the fundamentals of fractions. They compare the size of various halves, quarters, thirds, and so forth and notice that the size or number of parts to make a fraction can vary depending on the size of the whole.

Computer Activity

1. Students open the *Equivalent Fractions* template and follow the instructions.

2. In the first part of the lesson, students change the fill color or fill pattern of the correct number of cells to match the fraction above each block of cells. To do this, they highlight the cell or cells, click on the Fill Color or Fill Pattern button, and make a selection.

3. In the second part of the lesson, students describe the patterned areas in fractions above each block of cells. They need to enter each fraction in its lowest form.

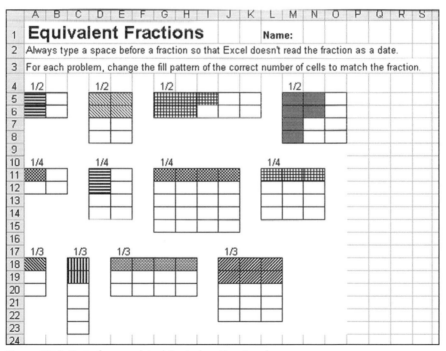

Figure 25.1. Part of a completed Equivalent Fractions lesson.

Colored Fractions

Exercise Description

In this fractions exercise, students learn that a whole can be divided into many parts of different sizes.

Computer Activity

1. Students open the *Colored Fractions* template.

2. In the first part of the lesson, students color the correct number of cells to match the fractions described below each block. To do this, they highlight the cell or cells, click on the Fill Color button and make a selection.

3. In the second part of the lesson, students color each block of cells as desired and type the fraction for each color below the block.

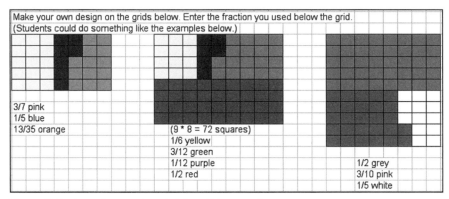

Figure 25.2. Part of a completed Colored Fractions lesson.

Fractions: Greater Than or Less Than?

Exercise Description

This exercise continues the lessons with fractions. Students learn that a unit of 40 cells can be divided equally into many parts—quarters, tenths, fifths, and so on—and that those parts may be added together to create different sizes. They also gain practice in comparing the size of fractions using the spreadsheet's visual cues.

Computer Activity

Student Instructions are provided, but most students will need guidance from the teacher as they work through the exercise.

1. Students open the *Greater or Less Than* template. Students are asked to count the number of cells in each row (the total is 40).

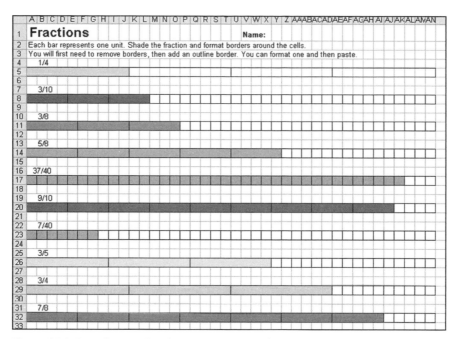

Figure 25.3. Part of a completed Fractions: Greater Than or Less Than? lesson.

2. They are also asked how many cells make half of 40.

3. Students seem to automatically understand this fraction, and give the correct answer of 20. Yet, they have problems generalizing this procedure to other fractions. An explanation like the following may help: How did you get the answer 20? By dividing 40 by the denominator, 2. It had to be divided into two parts.

4. To decide how many cells will be in next division, they proceed as they did above for a half. To get 1/4 of 40, they divide 40 by 4, which equals 10; therefore, 1/4 = 10 cells. They highlight 10 cells, format the borders of those cells, and then use the Copy and Paste features to divide the rest of the row into quarters. If they make a mistake and miscount it will be evident, as the portions will not fill all the way to the end of the bar.

5. After making the divisions, students shade 1/4 of the first row. They are instructed to tear away the Fill Color palette so that it is available for all the examples.

6. For the next row, 3/10, they first determine that 1/10 of 40 = 4 cells. They format borders for this row so that each tenth is outlined, and then color 3/10.

7. Students format and color all the fractions on the worksheet.

8. They use the Line tool to draw a line down through the halfway mark on all the bars.

9. The teacher checks the work and then the students print their worksheets.

10. Looking at the printout of their fractions, students add a sign to show whether the first fraction is greater than (>) or less than (<) the second fraction for the examples on their instruction sheet (3/10 < 3/8, 3/4 > 7/10, 7/40 < 1/4, 3/5 < 5/8).

Extensions

- The Greater Than or Lesser Than? lesson can be done with a whole divided into a different number, such as 30 or 35, and different fractions could be used, such as 1/3. To use this template, the teacher would highlight the desired number of cells, click on the File menu, select Print Area, and Set Print Area.

- Students can combine decimals and fractions on the same spreadsheet.

- Have students visit the National Council of Teachers of Mathematics Web site at http://standards.nctm.org/document/eexamples/chap5/5.1/index.htm. Here, students can play a game called Fraction Track to help them understand the relative size and equivalence of fractions. Students play with a partner. Using a table, they must move the dots along a number line to make as many fractions as possible equivalent to the number generated.

Fractions: Greater Than or Less Than?

Student Instructions

1. How many cells are in each row? _____

2. How many cells make half of 40? _____

3. How did you work this out? _____

4. Divide 40 into quarters.

   - 40 divided by 4 = 10, so 1/4 = 10 cells.

   - Format the borders of the first 10 cells. (Highlight the cells, click on the Format menu, select Cells, choose the Borders tab, and click on Outline.)

   - Use Copy and Paste to put the other quarters in the row.

   - All the cells in the row should now be in a quarter.

5. Fill one quarter with color.

   - Hold down your mouse on the Fill Color title bar, and drag it to tear it away to the right side of the screen so that the menu floats on the document.

   - Highlight one quarter of the first row.

   - Choose a color to fill the quarter.

6. Complete the next row, 3/10.

   - 1/10 of 40 = _____ cells.

   - Format borders for this row so that each tenth is outlined.

   - Color 3/10.

7. Continue to format and color all the fractions on the worksheet.

8. Use the Line tool to draw a line down through the halfway mark on all the bars. Click on the Line tool button on the Drawing Toolbar, position and hold down the mouse, and drag to draw a vertical line through the center of the bars. If you hold down the Shift key while you draw the line, it will be straight.

9. Have the teacher check your work and print it.

10. Using the fractions on your worksheet as a guide, add a sign to show whether the first fraction is greater than (>) or less than (<) the second fraction below:

3/10	3/8	7/40	1/4
3/4	7/10	3/5	5/8

26. Music Survey

Lesson Description

The class is asked if they think they have different taste in music than their parents. We brainstorm how to test whether there is in fact a difference in music tastes. The class conducts a survey to scientifically investigate their theories. We explore the idea of ranking types of music, and students form groups of two or three to discuss what types of music to include in the questionnaire. They then research types of music in an online encyclopedia like World Book or Encarta, and the class shares their ideas. They agree on the types of music to include, and using the *Music Survey Worksheet* (Figure 26.1), they write in seven types of music and a couple of examples for each type that interviewees will rank. Each student interviews three students at school and three adults at home. Students record their findings, organizing the information in a table. Interviewees rank the music types from most to least favorite, using ordinal numbers, where 1 is the highest ranking. They then share their data to get class totals for most favorite type of music for adults and children. We discuss how we can total our findings and decide to add the number of most favorites for students (1s). We do the same for the adult scores.

Higher-Order Thinking Skills	Spreadsheet Skills Practiced	Subject Areas and Standards Addressed
Solve the problem of collecting evidence to compare adult and student tastes in music	Move between Sheets 1, 2, and 3 on a spreadsheet document	NETS•S: 4
Identify and define different types of music. Listen to samples of the various types (appealing to auditory learners)	Highlight cells that are not adjacent using the Ctrl key	Mathematics: 5, 7
Develop a questionnaire	If you choose to make your own chart on a new spreadsheet:	Science: A1
Evaluate and rank the various types of music	■ Format borders	
Organize and analyze results for the students and for the adults surveyed	■ Insert a chart	
Compare findings for the two groups	■ Format a chart— gridlines, Y-axis, scale	
Create charts from scratch (this is optional) and interpret the charts		

Computer Activity

1. After agreeing on what types of music will be included in the survey, students write in seven types of music and examples for each type on the *Music Survey Worksheet*.

2. Students then conduct interviews, gathering answers from three students at school and three adults at home. Students ask the interviewees to rank the music types from most to least favorite, using ordinal numbers, where 1 is the highest ranking. Students record all responses on the *Music Survey Worksheet*.

3. Students can see the results of their own survey by organizing their finds in a table. This won't reveal much, however, so students should share their data to arrive at class totals for most favorite type of music for adults and children.

4. Students take turns entering their data on a single copy of *Music Survey–Class Data*, putting student data on Sheet 1 and adult data on Sheet 2.

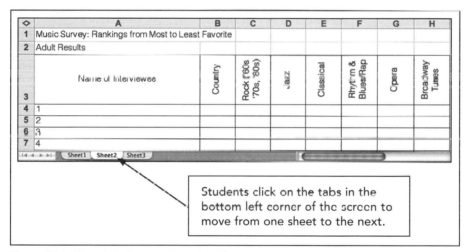

Figure 26.1. The adult data is collected on Sheet 2.

The computer automatically tallies the number of favorites (responses with a score of 1) and the number of least favorites (responses with a score of 7). The COUNTIF formula is used to count the rankings, as shown in figure 26.3, in cells B94 and B95. These totals are automatically transferred to Sheet 3.

| 94 | Class Total for Student Ranking of 1 | =COUNTIF(B4:B93,1) |
| 95 | Class Total for Student Ranking of 7 | =COUNTIF(B4:B93,7) |

Figure 26.2. The formulas in cells B94 and B95 transfer the totals to Sheet 3.

5. Print copies of the completed Sheet 3 for each student.

6. Each student individually follows the instructions on Sheet 3 to make a chart of the survey findings.

7. After making a chart, each student writes three sentences to interpret his or her findings.

To make the chart:

1. Open Excel, and a new, blank spreadsheet.

2. Using your copy of Sheet 3, enter the data from the class spreadsheet that they want to include in their chart that compares adult and student tastes in music.

3. Format borders around cells. Highlight the cells, then click on the Borders button on the Formatting toolbar.

 **Borders Icon**

4. Highlight the data you want to include in the chart, then click on the Insert menu, Chart, and then Finish. Figure 26.3 shows a sample of the completed lesson, formatted to make it easy to read.

If you want to print out a chart that looks like the sample and you do not wish to do the formatting, use the *Music Survey–Chart* template rather than a blank spreadsheet document.

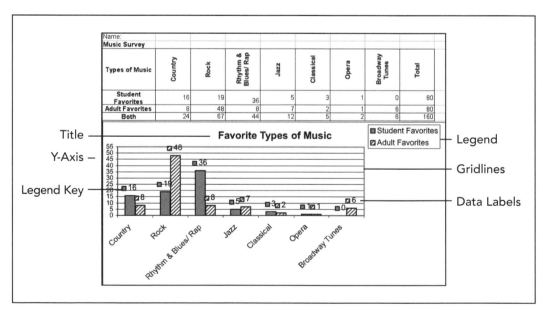

Figure 26.3. Totals automatically change as students enter data in Sheet 1 and Sheet 2.

To format the chart:

You can change the way a chart looks by double-clicking something you want to change, or by right-clicking it. The following instructions explain how the formatting was done on the chart in Figure 26.3:

1. After inserting the chart, right-click it, and click on Chart Options.

2. Click on the Titles tab and type in "Favorite Types of Music."

3. Click on the Gridlines tab and check Major Gridlines for the X-axis, and check Major Gridlines and Minor Gridlines for the Y-axis.

4. Click on the Legend tab, and select Show Legend and the placement you want for it—Top is selected in the example above.

5. Click on the Data Labels tab and select Show Value. Click on OK and the changes will appear on your chart.

6. Double-click on the Y-axis, and the Format Axis window pops up. Click on the Scale tab, and change the minor unit to 5, and if you like, change the maximum to 55. Click on OK to make these changes.

7. To change the color or pattern in the columns of the chart, click on the color you wish to change in the legend key, click on the Format menu, and choose Selected Legend Key. Choose the color and pattern you like. Click on OK and this changes the chart.

8. Double-click on any font size you wish to change and the Format Data Labels window will open. Click on the Font tab, and select the size and font you like.

9. Save and print your chart.

Extension

Students who complete the lesson quickly can make a chart using the data collected to determine the *least* favorite music for adults and students. They can use the lowest number of 1s or the highest number of 7 rankings to determine the least favorite choice.

27. States and Capitals

Lesson Description

Students use an online or print reference to check their knowledge of states. They use a map of the United States to help them unscramble the state names and practice spelling them correctly. Then they make flash cards to help them study states, capitals, and the two-letter postal abbreviations. They print the flash cards as a learning aid, and the checking feature of this lesson ensures that they do not learn from erroneous material. For help with some of the facts, students can visit the Factmonster Web site (www.factmonster.com) which has lists of states, capitals, and postal abbreviations.

Higher-Order Thinking Skills	Spreadsheet Skills Practiced	Subject Areas and Standards Addressed
Identify and recall information	Enter text in cells	NETS•S: 3 Social Studies: IIIa, c

Computer Activity

1. Students open the *States Jumbled* template and solve the word jumbles, all names of states.

2. Students open the *States Information* template and complete the table (columns B and C). Lists of state capitals and postal abbreviations are provided, and must be matched with the states. Students can visit Factmonster (www.factmonster. com) to check their work.

3. Students open the *States Flash Cards* template and create a set of flash cards to check knowledge of the states. The capitals and postal abbreviations in the spreadsheet are incorrect. Students arrange the information to be correct.

4. Have students check their answers on a map, then save and print their work.

5. Students can then cut out their flash cards and fold them on the dotted line. They can use them to test their knowledge of the state capitals and postal abbreviations.

◇	A	B
1	afordil	Florida
2	saxte	Texas
3	waio	Iowa
4	nsiiwsnco	Wisconsin
5	frinclaaio	California
6	setninoam	Minnesota
7	groeno	Oregon
8	snkaas	Kansas

Figure 27.1.
The *States Jumbled* template.

Our 50 States

Complete the columns B and C in the table below, matching the capitals and abbreviations to the states.
The capitals are listed in alphabetical order in column G, and the abbreviations are in column I. Once you match a capital to a state, delete it from the list. You must retype the information—do not drag and drop.

State	Capital	Abbreviation	Correct Capital	Correct Abbreviation	Capital	Abbreviation
Alabama	Montgomery	AL	1	1	Albany	AZ
Alaska			0	0	Annapolis	AK
Arizona			0	0	Atlanta	
Arkansas			0	0	Augusta	AR
California			0	0	Austin	CA
Colorado			0	0	Baton Rouge	CO
Connecticut			0	0	Bismarck	CT
Delaware			0	0	Boise	DE
Florida			0	0	Boston	FL
Georgia			0	0	Carson City	GA
Hawaii			0	0	Charleston	HI
Idaho			0	0	Cheyenne	IA
Illinois			0	0	Columbia	ID

Figure 27.2. The *States Information* template.

Extension

Ask any question in Column A. Delete unnecessary columns and rows by clicking on the column or row to highlight it, click on the Edit menu, and click on Delete. Modify the formulas in column D. The formula in cell D5 reads as follows: =IF(B5="Montgomery","1","0") Change it to =IF(B5="*type in correct answer here*","1","0") and it will score a 1 if that answer is put in B5. See "Getting Started with Spreadsheets" at the beginning of this book for more ideas on making self-scoring worksheets.

Fifth-Grade Lessons

28. **Science Dictionary** (SCIENCE)

29. **Decimals and Negatives** (MATH)

    - Decimals on a Grid

    - Decimals on a Number Line

    - Negative Numbers

30. **Finding Prime Numbers** (MATH)

31. **U.S. Weather Chart** (MATH, SCIENCE, SOCIAL STUDIES)

32. **Concept Maps: Fairy Tales** (LANGUAGE ARTS)

33. **Planning a Road Trip** (LANGUAGE ARTS, SOCIAL STUDIES, MATH)

28. Science Dictionary

Lesson Description

Students use the spreadsheet to enter words and their definitions, creating a dictionary that can be used for study. This lesson is effective when used in tandem with a unit in science or social studies. Students format column width, row height, and borders and sort alphabetically. They may continue to add words and sort them as they progress through a learning unit. This lesson provides a good way to review for a chapter or unit test.

This may be a good point to review with students how to customize the Formatting toolbar. See "Quick Reference Guide for Using Excel" at the beginning of this book for details.

Higher-Order Thinking Skills	Spreadsheet Skills Practiced	Subject Areas and Standards Addressed
Search online resources to define scientific terms; students explain them in their own words	Adjust column width and row height Enable text wrapping Format borders Sort words in alphabetical order	NETS•S: 3 Science: B

Computer Activity

1. Students open a new spreadsheet document and type the headings "Science Dictionary," "Vocabulary," and "Definition." *The Science Dictionary* template already has the headings entered.

2. If the Formatting toolbar is not showing, students click on the View menu and select Toolbars and check Formatting.

3. Students highlight the headings and change the font size to 18. They make fonts bold by using the Bold icon on the Formatting toolbar.

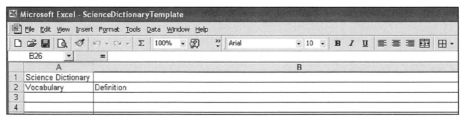

Figure 28.1. The Formatting toolbar provides the tools needed to set up a spelling dictionary.

4. They enter their name in the appropriate cell, then click on the cell again and use the Toolbar icon to right-align text.

5. Students type words and their definitions into the spreadsheet.

6. Students may find that their words and definitions aren't fitting in the space provided. They may change the column width and row height by dragging the mouse on the borders of the headings or by clicking on the Format menu and selecting Column Width or Row Height.

7. Students may also format alignment to allow words to fit by clicking on the Format menu, selecting Cell and the Alignment tab, and placing a check mark next to Wrap text.

8. Students format borders by highlighting a cell or cells, clicking on the Borders icon on the Formatting toolbar, and selecting All Borders.

9. To sort the words alphabetically, students highlight both columns, click on the Data menu, and select Sort.

10. Students continue adding new words and definitions. Then they sort alphabetically.

Extensions

- The teacher gives students the list of words and they find the definitions.

- The teacher provides a spreadsheet with words and definitions that do not correlate correctly with one another. Students need to insert a blank column between the two columns and move definitions to the correct place in the empty column using Cut and Paste. An example is given on the *Science Definitions–Match* sample (Figure 28.2). The teacher easily generates a template like the one in Figure 28.2 by typing in the target vocabulary words next to their definitions, then sorting one column only into alphabetical order.

◇	A	B
1	Science Definitions	
2	Insert a column between the two columns below.	
3	Cut each vocabulary word and paste it in the empty column next to its definition.	
4	Name:	
5		
6	Vocabulary	Definition
7	atom	A force that holds two atoms together
8	atomic number	A group of atoms held together by one type of chemical bond
9	chemical property	A particle that has a negative electric charge
10	chemical symbol	A particle that has no electric charge
11	compound	A particle that has a positive electric charge
12	electron	A substance made when two or more elements combine to form a new substance
13	element	Matter that contains two or more different substances
14	chemical bond	A trait that can be observed or measured without changing the identity of the substance
15	matter	A trait that describes how one substance reacts with another substance
16	metals	A way to describe how something looks or acts
17	mixture	An element that has no shine and cannot be shaped
18	model	An element that is a gas and does not react readily with other elements
19	molecule	An element that is shiny and can be rolled or pounded into various shapes
20	neutron	An element that has properties of both a metal and nonmetal

Figure 28.2.
In an extension to the Science Dictionary lesson, students match words to the correct definitions.

29. Decimals and Negatives

Lesson Description

Students often have problems conceptualizing decimal and negative numbers. The visual image of a grid or a number line on a spreadsheet produces a concrete representation of these abstract concepts as students compare the size of numbers. This lesson is made up of three exercises: Decimals on a Grid, Decimals on a Number Line, and Negative Numbers.

Higher-Order Thinking Skills	Spreadsheet Skills Practiced	Subject Areas and Standards Addressed
Connect visual representation on a number line and the abstract concept of decimals and negative numbers Compare and discriminate between decimal numbers, arrange them in order Invent new decimals and negative numbers, find a new way to show these numbers	Enter numbers Fill cells with color Add arrows using the Arrow tool Change the color of text	NETS•S: 6 Mathematics: 1, 3

Decimals on a Grid

Exercise Description

As students begin to understand decimals, it helps them to graphically represent them by shading an area on a grid and by describing the shaded area using decimal numbers.

Computer Activity

1. Students open the *Decimals on a Grid* template.

2. The teacher discusses what fraction of the whole is shaded and how that fraction can be represented by a decimal. Students are reminded that we do not write 0.1 as 0.10, although it represents 10 shaded parts in a unit divided into 100. Each grid block is made up of 100 tiny squares, and each group of 100 tiny squares represents one whole number.

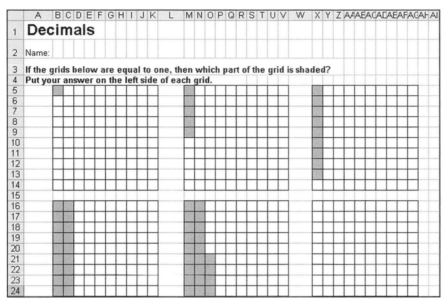

Figure 29.1. The *Decimals on a Grid* template.

3. In the first part of this lesson, students describe the shaded area on the template in decimals. They place their answer to the left of each grid. This visual representation helps clarify the difference between 0.01 and 0.1.

4. In the second part of this lesson, students shade the correct number of cells to illustrate the given decimal. They highlight a cell or cells and change the color using the Fill Color button on the Formatting toolbar. Holding down the Ctrl key enables a student to shade a whole row and part of a row at the same time. It is not necessary to print this lesson.

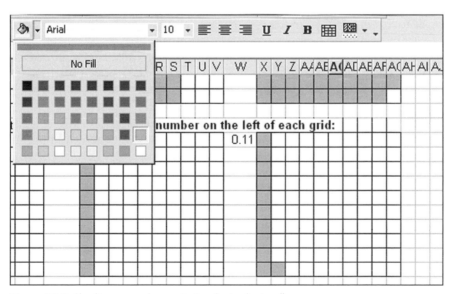

Figure 29.2. Shading areas demonstrates decimals visually.

Decimals on a Number Line

Exercise Description

Placing decimals on a number line helps students visualize the meaning and size of decimal numbers. The graphical representation of the number line also helps students understand the concepts of greater than and less than.

Computer Activity

1. The teacher opens the *Decimals Demo* template and reviews with the class how whole numbers and decimals are ordered on a number line. The teacher demonstrates on the spreadsheet how one unit (1.0) can be divided into decimals (0.1, 0.2, etc.), then how 0.1 can be divided into smaller decimals, and so on to infinity. The numbers 1.5 and 2 can be seen by using the Scroll bar at the bottom of the screen.

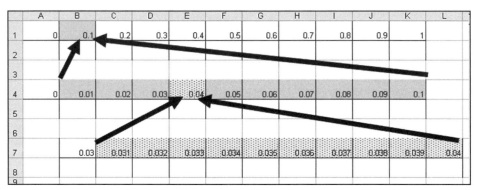

Figure 29.3. The *Decimals Demo* template is a good place to start the Decimals on a Line lesson.

2. Students open the *Decimals on a Line* template and follow instructions to enter numbers on the number line. On the first number line they enter tenths, on the second they enter hundredths, and on the third they enter both. This helps clarify the meaning of decimals. The font color has been formatted in red for numbers students enter so that these stand out and can be easily checked.

3. Students use the Arrow tool on the Drawing toolbar to show exactly where the decimal numbers lie. They click on the button, then drag the mouse to make a line.

4. The next activity involves a different spreadsheet. Students open the *Number Line* template.

5. They place numbers on the number line. They change the text color by highlighting numbers and clicking on the Font Color button on the Formatting toolbar. They use the Arrow tool to show exactly where the decimal numbers lie.

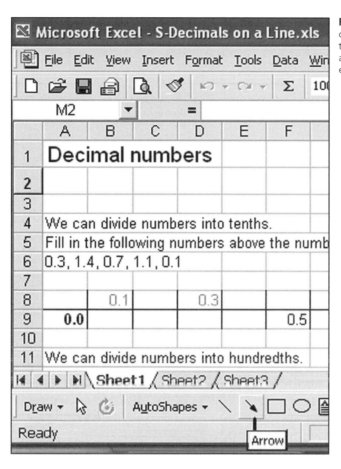

Figure 29.4. Click on the Arrow tool to add an arrowhead to the end of a line.

6. Students then add the appropriate sign, greater than (>) or less than (<), between pairs of numbers the teacher provides, such as the following:

0.8	0.99
0.8	0.75
1800	950
0.9	0.99

Negative Numbers

Exercise Description

After students have been introduced to the concept of negative numbers, they place positive and negative numbers on a number line. A visual representation will help students understand the concept of negative numbers. Instructions are on the template.

Computer Activity

1. Students open the *Negative Numbers* template.

2. Students follow the directions on the template, placing positive and negative numbers on the number line.

Extension

Students are given a different set of numbers and asked to enter them on a number line in a new spreadsheet document, without using a template. Have them follow these instructions to create a number line on a new spreadsheet:

1. Format borders to show the number line and intersecting lines.

2. Highlight the row where you want the line to appear. Pull down the Format menu, click on Cells, and select the Borders tab.

3. Click on Inside, and click on OK.

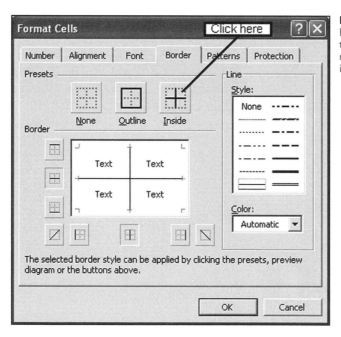

Figure 29.5.
Format borders to show the number line and intersecting lines.

30. Finding Prime Numbers

Lesson Description

Before doing this lesson, students should have learned multiples and factors and understand the difference between a prime and composite number. (A prime number has only two factors, 1 and itself.)

Students enter the numbers 1 through 100 on the grid, using formulas to enter numbers, and using Fill Right and Fill Down to generalize those formulas. They underline the prime numbers and black out all the composite numbers, leaving only prime numbers. This exercise reinforces students' understanding of prime numbers.

Higher-Order Thinking Skills	Spreadsheet Skills Practiced	Subject Areas and Standards Addressed
Formulate a way for the computer to count to 100 Analyze what defines a prime number Compare and distinguish between primes and composites	Create and enter formulas Extend formulas using Fill Right and Fill Down Show formulas or data Fill cells with color Underline text	NETS•S: 3 Mathematics: 1, 2, 3

Computer Activity

See the Student Instructions on the next page, "Finding Prime Numbers."

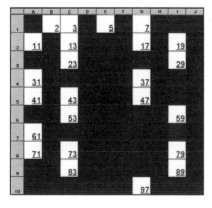

Figure 30.1.
The Sieve of Eratosthenes "drains" composite numbers, leaving prime numbers behind.

Finding Prime Numbers
Student Instructions

USE FORMULAS TO COUNT TO 100

1. Open a new spreadsheet document.

2. Enter the number 1 in cell A1.

3. To enter a formula, click in the cell where you want your answer (B1). Click on = (the equal sign) to let the computer know that a formula is being entered. Click on the cell you want to add 1 to (A1). Type in +1. The formula is =A1+1. Press the Enter key and the answer will appear in the cell.

4. To extend the formula to the right, highlight the cell containing the formula you have made (B1), hold down the mouse, and drag across the cells you want to fill with that formula (highlight all the way to J1). Click on the Edit menu, select Fill, and choose Right.

5. Cell A2 must be equal to 10 more than cell A1, so the formula in A2 is =A1+10. Extend the formula to the right by highlighting the cell containing the formula (A2), holding down the mouse, and dragging across the cells you want to fill with that formula (highlight all the way to J2). Click on the Edit menu, select Fill, and choose Right.

6. To extend the formula down, highlight the cell containing the formula, hold down the mouse, and drag down over the cells you want to fill with that formula. Highlight the cells in row 2 (A2..J2) and hold the mouse down until all the cells through J10 are highlighted. Click on the Edit menu, select Fill, and choose Down.

7. Click on the Tools menu, select Options, choose the View tab, and place a check mark next to Formulas.

8. Click on the Tools menu, select Options, choose the View tab, and remove the check mark next to Formulas to view the data.

9. Save the 100s chart as "Prime Numbers."

continued

Finding Prime Numbers
Student Instructions continued

FIND PRIME NUMBERS

1. Use the Sieve of Eratosthenes to find all the prime numbers on this chart. Eratosthenes invented a "sieve" that you could use to "drain" or delete the composite numbers and leave the prime numbers behind. You will fill all the cells that contain a composite number with black and underline all primes.

   ■ Click on the View menu and select Toolbars. Add a check mark next to Formatting, so that the Fill Color button will be available.

   ■ The number 1 is not prime, so fill it with black. Highlight cell A1, click on the Fill Color button, and choose the color black.

   ■ The first prime number is 2. Underline it. Use the U button on the Button bar. Count by 2s and fill every cell containing a multiple of 2 with black.

   ■ The next prime number is 3. Underline it. Count by 3s and fill every cell containing a multiple of 3 with black. If a number is already blackened out it should be a multiple of 2 and 3.

   ■ The next prime number is 5. Underline it. Count by 5s and fill every cell containing a multiple of 5 with black.

   ■ Repeat the steps until all the numbers in the chart have either been underlined or blackened out. The remaining (underlined) numbers are the prime numbers from 1 to 100.

2. Click on the View menu, select Header and Footer, click on Custom Footer, and type in your name and the date. Save and print.

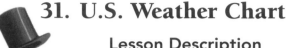

31. U.S. Weather Chart

Lesson Description

Students use the Internet or a newspaper to monitor temperatures across the U.S. for a week. They enter the temperatures in a spreadsheet and use the spreadsheet tools to calculate the average temperature for the week and generate graphs. They also record precipitation and make a chart to compare it for different locations, including both rainfall and snowfall data. Looking at the graphs, they discuss the range of temperatures and precipitation, and why the weather would be different in different regions. They identify the places with the highest and lowest temperatures, and highest and lowest precipitation for the week. They decide which type of graph would convey most clearly the information they want to share about the temperature and precipitation in different places. From the Internet or newspaper they print or clip weather maps for the week showing high and low pressure fronts. The Weather Underground Web site (www.wunderground.com) is useful for accessing historic temperatures for the last five days and predicted temperatures for the next five days.

Students examine the weather maps and try to explain the temperature range and variations in precipitation levels across the country. Factors such as distance from the equator and altitude are discussed, and daily the class examines high and low pressure areas, warm and cold fronts, and how they affect conditions. Weather maps for the U.S. are examined daily at this site, and may be printed for reference in the classroom. Online they can be expanded, and animated. As an Extension, students can record predicted temperatures and precipitation for the week, and after the week is over, compare these to actual temperatures. They can also examine factors like the wind speed for their hometown, and compare this to a different location. There are several charts online that they can analyze to make their comparisons.

Higher-Order Thinking Skills	Spreadsheet Skills Practiced	Subject Areas and Standards Addressed
Create graphs to represent recorded data found online	Enter data collected	NETS•S: 3, 4
Organize data	Calculate averages using formulas	Mathematics: 3, 5, 6, 10
Examine and interpret the facts in terms of weather knowledge	Extend a formula using Fill Down	Science: D
Communicate findings	Format numbers as fixed numbers	Social Studies: IIIf
	Make charts	
	Resize and move charts	

Computer Activity

1. Using the Internet or the daily newspaper, the class monitors daily temperatures and precipitation for five days in the cities listed on the *US Weather* template. If you miss a day, and want to find a history of the weather, look for the city you want on the Weather Underground Web site (www.wunderground.com), then scroll down to History and Almanac, and select the appropriate date.

2. Students open the *US Weather* template and enter their data.

3. Starting with Chicago, students use Excel's ready-made functions to calculate the average temperature. After selecting cell G6, they pull down the Insert menu and select Function, then Statistical under Categories, and finally choose Average. This inserts a formula in the cell.

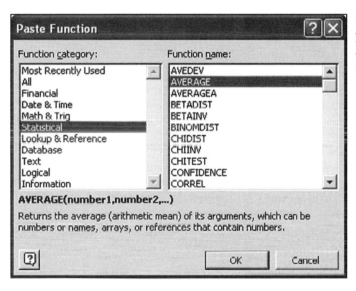

Figure 31.1.
A formula to find the average temperatures can easily be inserted.

The formula reads as follows: =AVERAGE(B7:F7) where the cell addresses in parentheses show the range of cells to be averaged. The computer "guesses" which cells you want to average, but this can be changed by highlighting the cell numbers between parentheses and dragging over the cells you want to average.

4. To extend this formula down, students click on G7, hold down the mouse, and drag cursor to G15. They click on the Edit menu and select Fill Down.

5. The numbers that appear in the average column need formatting. Have students highlight column G, click on the Format menu, and select Cell, then the Number tab, click on Number, and choose the desired number of decimal places.

6. To make a chart, students highlight cells A6 to A15, hold down the Ctrl key and highlight cells G6 to G15, so that non-adjacent cells will be highlighted. They click on the Insert menu, and on Chart. They select the type of chart they wish to make by clicking on Column and then on Finish. The column graph appears on the spreadsheet document.

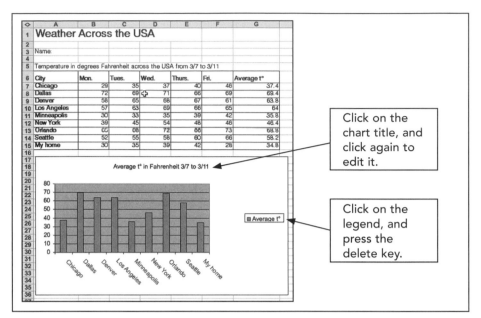

Click on the chart title, and click again to edit it.

Click on the legend, and press the delete key.

Figure 31.2. A sample completed US Weather lesson.

7. Students double-click on the bar graph title, "Average t°City," and change it to "Average Temperature in Fahrenheit 3/7 to 3/11."

8. Students may want to move or resize their charts. To move, place the mouse in the middle of the chart, hold down the mouse, and drag. To resize, click on the chart, hold down the mouse on one of the corners, and drag.

9. Have students repeat the steps above to calculate average precipitation for the five days, and then chart it.

10. Teachers and students examine the weather maps and talk about the causes of the temperature and precipitation range across the country, considering factors like high and low pressure areas, and movement of cold and warm fronts.

Extensions

- The teacher can modify the list of places on the template: select different cities in the U.S. or worldwide, possibly cities that have been prominent in current events or that have had weather disasters recently. Students chart average temperatures and precipitation for the places, remembering to hold down Ctrl to chart non-adjacent cells.

- Students can record predicted temperatures for the week. After the week is over, they compare this data to actual temperatures and discuss the accuracy of weather forecasts. Have them explore the data meteorologists use to make predictions, and try to explain some of their miscalculations.

- Sunrise time and sunset time may be recorded for each location. Students examine and explain how the days get longer and which places on the map have daylight for longer hours.

32. Concept Maps: Fairy Tales

Lesson Description

Excel can be used to create concept maps for making comparisons and determining causal relationships. Excel is the perfect tool for making concept maps that are arranged in linear fashion—using cells arranged on the grid simplifies visual layout. Older students can easily modify a template or create their own concept maps with the help of written instructions and demonstration by the teacher. In the following lesson, fifth-grade students write a different version of a story they have read using a concept map in Excel.

Higher-Order Thinking Skills	Spreadsheet Skills Practiced	Subject Areas and Standards Addressed
Organize information	Enter text	NETS•S: 3, 4
Compare and contrast ideas	Resize column width	Language Arts: 5
Identify causal relationships	Insert and delete cells	
	Move arrows	

Computer Activity

1. Students read a story, then open the *Fairy Tale* template.

2. Students enter text in the template's spreadsheet cells, rewriting the familiar story. The borders have been formatted for them. The template is formatted for landscape printing—students can change the column width to expand the cell size as needed. To resize column width, click on the border between the column headings and drag. Or, select more than one column at a time by clicking on the first to select it, hold down Ctrl, and click on the second and third to select them also. Click on the Format menu, and on Column Width. Have students experiment with the number to get the width they like.

3. Students may find it necessary to add cells as they flesh out their stories. To insert cells, have them click where they want to insert the cell. Click on the Insert menu and on Cells. To delete cells, they can click on the cell or cells they want to delete, then click on the Edit menu and on Delete. Students can also use drag and drop to move cells on the grid.

4. Students modify the template to suit, such as changing the fonts and filling cells with color.

5. Students may also wish to add clip art to their story. To insert clip art, have students click on the Insert Clip Art icon on the Drawing toolbar, search for a picture by entering a name in the search bar, or browse a category. They then click on the clip art they want to insert, then click on Insert Clip. They can

resize the picture by holding down the mouse on the handle bar and dragging. Pictures float on top of cells and can easily be moved around. Move the picture by holding down the mouse in the middle of the picture and dragging.

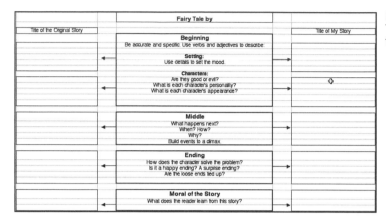

Figure 32.1.
The *Fairy Tale* template.

6. If an arrow is no longer in the right place, students simply click on it and drag it to the desired position. To select more than one arrow at a time, have them click on the first arrow, then press Shift and click on the additional arrow or arrows. To delete an arrow, have students click on it so that the handlebars show, and press the delete key on the keyboard.

7. Students can insert comments to add detailed notes behind main ideas. These will only show up when the cursor is placed over a cell. To insert a comment, students right-click on the cell, left-click on Insert Comment, and type in the text they want to hide behind the cell.

Extensions

- Students explore relationships as they plan a cause-and-effect essay, such as how eating too much affects weight gain, or how practicing regularly can result in winning a competition. Students use the *Cause & Effect* template to map out their approach and collect their ideas.

- Students make their own concept maps in Excel (see Student Instructions).

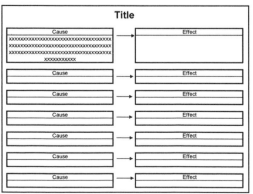

Figure 32.2.
The *Cause & Effect* template is shown as it will print, with only the formatted borders showing.

Making a Concept Map in Excel
Student Instructions

Use Excel to make your own concept map. Start with a blank spreadsheet.

To add a border around cells. Select the cell or cells, and click on the Borders button on the Formatting toolbar. Click on Outside Borders to put a border around a group of cells, or on Borders to put a border around an individual cell.

To move a cell or group of cells. Click on the cell border, hold down the mouse, and drag it to a desired location.

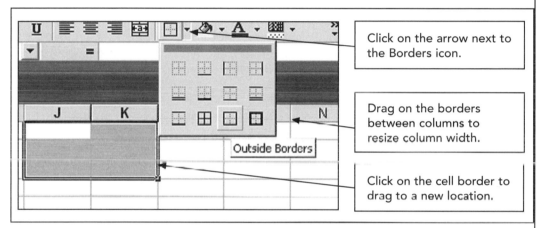

Click on the arrow next to the Borders icon.

Drag on the borders between columns to resize column width.

Click on the cell border to drag to a new location.

Figure 32.3. A concept map can be created in Excel.

To insert clip art. Click on the Insert Clip Art icon on the Drawing toolbar, search for a picture by entering a word or name in the search bar, or by browsing a category. Click on the clip art you want to insert, click on Insert Clip. Resize clip art by holding down the mouse on the handlebar and dragging, and move by holding down the mouse in the middle of the picture and dragging. Pictures float on top of cells and can easily be moved around.

To fill a cell with color. Click on the cell or cells to select them, click on the arrow next to the Fill Color button on the Drawing or Formatting toolbar, and select your color.

To widen a column. Click on the border between the column headings and drag, or select more than one column at a time by clicking on the first to select it, then hold down Ctrl, then click on the second and third to select them also. Click on the Format menu, and on Column Width. Experiment with the number to get the width you like.

continued

Making a Concept Map in Excel
Student Instructions continued

To widen a row. Click on the border between the row headings and drag, or select more than one column at a time by clicking on the first to select it, then hold down Ctrl, then click on the second and third to select them also. Click on the Format menu, and on Row Height. Experiment with the number to get the width you like.

To insert an arrow. Use the Arrow button on the Drawing toolbar to draw an arrow, and hold down the shift key to make the arrows perfectly straight. Select an arrow and hold down the Ctrl key and D to duplicate an arrow. Press Delete to delete it.

To insert a comment. To add more detailed notes behind main ideas, right-click the cell, left-click on Insert Comment, and type in the text you want to hide behind the cell. This will show up when the mouse is moved over the cell.

To insert links to other files or to Web pages. Right-click a cell and left-click on Hyperlink.

To merge or join together adjacent cells. To join cells next to, above, or below one another, click on a cell to select it, click on the Format menu, and on Cell, then on Alignment, and place a check mark next to Merge. To separate cells, repeat this step and remove the check mark next to Merge.

To wrap text. Click on a cell to select it, click on the Format menu, and on Cells and Alignment, and place a check mark next to Wrap Text to stop the text from spilling over into an adjacent cell.

To see how the spreadsheet will print. Click on the File menu, and on Print Preview.

33. Planning a Road Trip

Lesson Description

Students plan a road trip across the state or country, leaving from and returning to their hometown. They use the *Road Trip* template to capture the details of their itinerary. They visit Web sites about their chosen destinations, and use an Internet map service to find the distances they will travel. Finally, they make a poster about their trip.

Higher-Order Thinking Skills	Spreadsheet Skills Practiced	Subject Areas and Standards Addressed
Plan a trip and evaluate which places to visit Review Web resources, analyze information, and make decisions	Input data collected from an Internet site onto a spreadsheet Use an Internet map service to calculate distances between points Work in an Internet browser and Excel simultaneously	NETS•S: 6 English Language Arts: 8 Social Studies: IIIa–d

Computer Activity

1. Break the students into groups of two or three, and have them decide on a road trip itinerary across the state or country by looking at a map of major highways. Their itinerary should be a round trip, leaving from and returning to their hometown.

Road Trip

Name:
Directions: Plan a road trip. Use a search engine to research your trip. Enter the details of your itinerary in the table below.
Web Sites Visited: *(Paste the URLs of sites you used in your research below.)*

You can change the names under **Name of Place** to any destination in or near the place you live that you would like to visit, but you must end your journey back in your home town.

Name of Place	Last Place Visited	Mileage to Get There	Places to See	Places to Stay
	Starting Point			

Ending Point
Total Mileage Traveled

Write three sentences describing where you will go on your road trip, and why:
1
2
3

Figure 33.1. The *Road Trip* template.

2. After deciding where they want to travel, students use a search engine to find useful Web sites about their trip destinations. They should use this information to determine places to see and where to stay in each place, entering this information in the *Road Trip* template. While researching their trip, they can then modify their list of places to visit based on the information they find.

3. To complete the "Mileage to Get There" column, students access an online map service that provides driving directions, such as MapQuest, Google, or Yahoo Maps. They use this online site to calculate distances from one destination to the next.

4. Students should record the Web address of each research site they use in the *Road Trip* template. They can work in both programs simultaneously by minimizing the Excel window (click on the Minimize button in the top right corner of the window), opening an Internet browser window to search for information, then minimizing the browser window. To return to an open window, they click on it in the Task bar. Alternatively, students can press Alt and Tab then tab to switch between programs.

5. After completing their table, students print out a map from one of the map sites that shows all the places they will visit. They mark their road trip route on the map.

6. As a final activity, each student group makes a poster about their trip, showing the map, mileage table, and pictures of attractions that they print from the Internet. This may be done on poster board, or PowerPoint may be used to make a slideshow displaying the information.

Extensions

- Have students calculate the cost of traveling, such as staying at hotels, eating at restaurants, and visiting attractions. They enter this information on a spreadsheet and calculate a total cost for the trip. If they have a budget, they can modify their trip so as not to exceed the targeted amount.

- Use this lesson to learn about a foreign country, with students presenting their findings in a PowerPoint slideshow. Depending on their level of proficiency, they can ask and answer questions in the target language, or narrate the slideshow in that language.

Sixth-Grade Lessons

34. **Colored Candies:
Ratio, Percentage, and Estimation** (MATH)

35. **Foreign Language Dictionary** (LANGUAGE ARTS)

36. **Using Formulas to Calculate Equations** (MATH)

   - Using Formulas to Make Basic Calculations

   - Using Formulas to Evaluate Mathematical Expressions

   - Using Formulas to Solve Mathematical Equations

37. **Travel Slideshow** (MATH)

38. **Analyzing Complex Patterns** (MATH)

39. **Probability with Coins and Dice** (MATH)

40. **Comparing Countries** (SOCIAL STUDIES, MATH)

34. Colored Candies: Ratios, Percentage, and Estimation

Lesson Description

Students each receive a bag of colored candies and count the number of each color. M&M's were used in this lesson, but other colored candies would work just as well. In groups of three, students calculate the average number of candies of each color for their small group. They calculate the ratio of the number of each color to the total number of candies (for example, 28 blue out of 123 total) and compute that as a percentage. The information is used to make a pie chart.

Data for the entire class is also compiled. Students make a spreadsheet with the class data and calculate the average number of candies of each color for the entire class. Throughout the lesson, students are asked to make predictions about the amount of each color in the "mystery bag," first using their data, then their group's findings, and finally the data for the whole class. The mystery bag is then opened. Students examine which estimation is the most accurate and discuss probability.

The author would like to thank Mequon-Thiensville District Technology Department for sharing their ideas on this lesson.

Higher-Order Thinking Skills	Spreadsheet Skills Practiced	Subject Areas and Standards Addressed
Analyze data and compare results Use data to generalize and predict contents of the mystery bag Create and interpret a visual representation of ratios, averages, and percentages	Enter data collected Calculate averages and ratios using formulas Format numbers as percentages Make charts Search for information on the Internet (Extension)	NETS•S: 4 Mathematics: 5, 6, 9, 10

Computer Activity

1. Students form groups of three. They enter color totals for their bags and their group's bags on the *M&M's Predictions* template, and make a chart representing their data. They make predictions of color totals for a mystery bag of M&M's throughout the lesson. See Student Instructions for detailed directions.

2. The teacher supervises as students enter data for their own bags of M&M's on the *M&M's-Class* template. When all students have entered their data, the M&M's-Class spreadsheet is saved. Each group receives a copy of the spreadsheet (a digital copy on floppy disk or CD-ROM, or through the school network, or a hard copy).

3. Students enter the class totals on their own spreadsheets. Students make a new chart with the class data (Figure 34.1). Data has been entered, ratios calculated, and charts made.

4. Depending on students' mathematical abilities and their experience with spreadsheets, some discussion of how to answer the questions, a demonstration of how to do the lesson, or a printed copy of the completed lesson may be necessary. It is assumed that students already know how to make a chart (see U.S. Weather lesson). Some groups may not be able to make up the formulas for themselves and may need a printed copy of the sample lesson showing formulas.

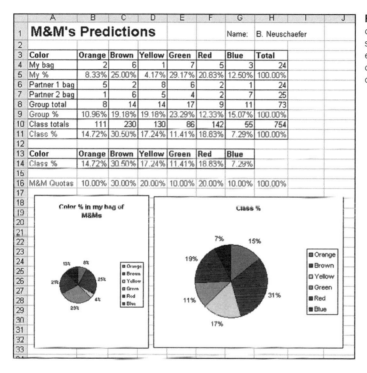

Figure 34.1. A completed lesson showing data entered, ratios calculated, and charts made.

Extensions

- Have students calculate the discrepancy between predicted and actual numbers of colored candies. They can do this on a spreadsheet.

- Have students predict the total number of M&M's in each bag. Hint: To get the average total per bag, divide the total of all the numbers in each bag by the number of people in the whole class.

- Have students compare their findings to Mars, Inc.'s, official quotas. For M&M's Milk Chocolate candies, the official quota is: 24% blue, 20% orange, 16% green, 14% yellow, 13% red, 13% brown. Students can make a chart to compare the official percentages with the calculations for the entire class.

- Have students work out the highest number, lowest number, and range for each set of data—the student's own bag, their group's findings, and the data for the class.

Colored Candies
Student Instructions

1. Form groups of three.

2. Open your own bag of M&M's and count the number of each color.

3. Open the *M&M's Predictions* template.

4. Type the number of candies of each color and the total in row 2.

5. Enter a formula in cell B3 to calculate the ratio of the color to the whole.

6. To format this number as a percentage, highlight the cell, click on the Format menu, click on Cells, and select the Number tab, and check Percentage.

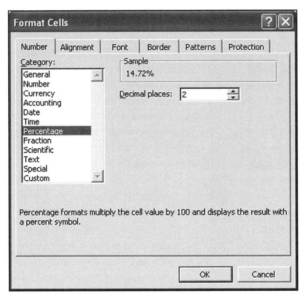

Example.
To format a number as a percentage, use the Format Cells menu.

7. To extend this formula to the right, highlight cell B3, drag the mouse right to G3, click on the Edit menu, and then on Fill, and on Right.

8. Make a chart called "Color Percentage in My Bag" to show your findings. (Highlight adjacent cells, click on the Insert menu, and select Chart.)

9. Given the data for your bag, what number of each color do you predict in the mystery bag?

First Prediction:

_____

continued

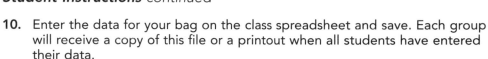

Colored Candies

Student Instructions continued

10. Enter the data for your bag on the class spreadsheet and save. Each group will receive a copy of this file or a printout when all students have entered their data.

11. On your own spreadsheet, in rows 4 and 5, enter the number of M&M's of each color for the bags belonging to the other members of your group.

12. Add the number of each color in rows 2, 4 and 5 to get a group total for each color. Put the group total for each color in row 6.

13. Calculate the group percentages in row 7.

14. How do these percentages differ from the calculations you made using your data only?

15. Given the data for your group, what number of each color do you predict in the mystery bag?

    Second Prediction:

    _____

16. The teacher will provide you with the class totals. Enter these in row 8.

17. Calculate the class percentages in row 9.

18. The data and the labels need to be selected so that they can be charted. To highlight rows that are not adjacent, click in a cell to select it, hold down your mouse and drag it to select other cells in that row, hold down the Ctrl key on the keyboard, and click-and-drag in a second row.

19. Using data from the class totals, rows 9 and 11, make a chart.

20. Compare your percentages to those of the class and comment:

    _____

21. Given the data for the whole class, what number of each color do you predict in the mystery bag?

    Third Prediction:

    _____

22. Save and print your spreadsheet and charts.

23. The teacher will open the mystery bag and share the color totals.

24. Which was the best predictor—your data, your group's data, or the data for the whole class? Why?

    _____

35. Foreign Language Dictionary

Lesson Description

English-speaking students who learn French sometimes struggle to learn new vocabulary and to distinguish between masculine and feminine words. Adding visual cues with clip art and changing the font color of masculine words to blue and feminine words to pink gives them a visual cue to help them learn the word with its gender.

Students make a dictionary and add clip art, translations into English, or synonyms, depending on their level of proficiency in the target language. The sample French dictionary was created for students who have recently learned weather and animal vocabulary. Students could make their own dictionaries or the teacher could make one and mix up the words, such as the French words on the *Foreign Language Dictionary* template provided. Students then rearrange the words in alphabetical order and place pictures next to matching words.

Higher-Order Thinking Skills	Spreadsheet Skills Practiced	Subject Areas and Standards Addressed
Use visual cues to sort feminine and masculine words Connect words with pictures	Insert a column between cells Move clip art Copy and paste text	NETS•S: 3 Foreign Language: 1.2

Computer Activity

1. Students open the *Foreign Language Dictionary* template.

◇	A	B	C	D	E	F	G	H	I	J
1	Vocabulaire			Name:						
2										
3	1. Retype the words in column B into alphabetical order in column C: ignore "le" and "la."									
4	2. Highlight column B.									
5	3. Click on the Edit menu and click on Delete.									
6	4. Match each picture with its meaning and move it next to the correct word by holding down the mouse and dragging.									
7	5. Change the color of feminine words to red and the masculine words to blue.									
8	6. When finished, delete these instructions.									
9										
10		le soleil								
11		le chien								
12		l'araignée								
13		la neige								
14		le cheval								

Figure 35.1. The *Foreign Language Dictionary* template.

2. They highlight column B, click on the Insert menu, and select Column to insert a blank column between the words and pictures.

3. Students then highlight one word, click on the Edit menu, and select Copy.

4. They move the cursor to where they want to paste the word, click on the Edit menu, and select Paste. Students need reminding that any text that was previously in the cell will be replaced by the new word.

5. Students paste the words in alphabetical order in the empty column. Or, if the teacher wants students to practice spelling, they type the words again without using Copy and Paste, following the instructions on the template. Students cannot use the Sort feature, as this sorts by the definite article, "le" or "la."

6. When all the words have been arranged alphabetically, students delete the column with words in the wrong order.

7. Students move the correct picture next to the word that matches its meaning.

8. They change the text color of masculine words to blue and feminine words to red by clicking on the appropriate cell to select it, and then clicking on the Font Color icon on the Formatting toolbar, or the arrow next to it to select a color of choice.

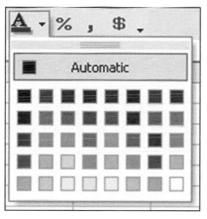

Figure 35.2.
Students use the Font Color icon to make masculine words blue and feminine words red.

Insert foreign language accents on a PC by using the Character Map:

A. Click on the Start menu and select Programs, Accessories, System Tools, and Character Map.

B. Change the font to match the font used in the document.

C. Copy the desired character by double-clicking on it and selecting Copy.

D. Click back on the document, select the Edit menu, and choose Paste.

E. Keyboard shortcuts can also be used. These are displayed on the bottom right corner of the Character Map window.

Extensions

- This lesson can be modified for a different target language, such as Spanish or German. For words in German, for which there is masculine, feminine, and neuter, three font colors could be used.

- Students are given a list of words. They change the font color according to gender and enter the meanings in their native tongue or find pictures to show their meanings.

36. Using Formulas to Calculate Equations

Lesson Description

Students use the spreadsheet to make a calculator. The lesson begins with a discussion about the functions of a calculator. Students are asked to identify the signs that may be used to make formulas in a spreadsheet calculator:

+   plus

–   minus

*   multiply

/   divide

^   to the power of (shift 6)

The class follows the Student Instructions to write formulas to make a calculator. Students may work with a partner to make up the necessary formulas. Simple numbers are included on the template so that they can check whether their formulas work. Class members print two copies of the Using Formulas to Make Basic Calculations lesson, one with formulas showing and one with data showing. Students use the calculator as a tool to make more complex calculations as they change the numbers.

Higher-Order Thinking Skills	Spreadsheet Skills Practiced	Subject Areas and Standards Addressed
Develop an understanding of how formulas can be used to perform operations: add, subtract, multiply, divide, and to the power of Write algebraic formulas to make a calculator and to perform operations Connect abstract variables with concrete examples Make predictions and analyze changes when seed values and formulas are modified Modify the starting value of a variable, the increment, and the formula to make calculations and see how that changes values	Adjust column width and row height Make up and insert a formula Fill a formula right or down Format numbers to one decimal place Format numbers as currency Insert a chart Use a function to calculate the absolute value of a number Use Auto Formatting to Fill Right for months of the year	NETS•S: 3 Mathematics: 2, 6

Using Formulas to Make Basic Calculations

The author would like to thank Mequon-Thiensville District Technology Department for sharing their ideas on this lesson.

Computer Activity

See Student Instructions for detailed directions. After the students complete the lesson, the teacher may discuss the final step with them and give the class calculations to do using the calculator.

After students print the lesson, the instructor should lead the class through the final four steps.

1. Explore how rounding off a number affects the answer.

2. Students use their spreadsheet to calculate the sum of 6.4 and 7.6.

3. What is the answer? Why is it not 14?

4. The teacher gives students other calculations to do using the calculator.

Using Formulas to Make Basic Calculations
Student Instructions

1. Look at the number pad and the top row of keys on the keyboard and add a sign for the following:

   plus _____   multiply _____

   minus _____   divide _____

   to the power of _____

   to let the computer know that a formula follows _____

2. Open the *Calculator* template.

3. Make headings bold by highlighting, holding down the Control key, and pressing B.

4. Adjust the size of the rows and columns using the mouse. Move the pointer to the border of the row or column heading until you see the double arrow pointer. Hold down the mouse and drag the border until the row or column is the right size, or double-click on the line between the column headers and it will automatically size. You can also click on Format, select Column/Row, and choose AutoFit Selection.

5. Enter formulas to make the calculations in the answer cells. Type in =, followed by the appropriate formula. Remember to use order of operations in the examples with two operations. Press the Enter key after putting in a formula. Use the Esc key to get out of a cell where a formula has gone wrong.

6. Some answers may be decimal numbers. Format the numbers in the answer cells by highlighting E1 through E8, click on the Format menu, select Cells, and choose the Number tab. Click on Number and choose 1 for Decimal Places.

7. Repeat for cells G11 through G12.

8. Print twice, once showing formulas and once showing data. To show formulas, click on Tools, select Options or Preferences, choose the View tab, and place a check mark next to Formulas. To show data, follow the same procedure but remove the check mark next to Formulas.

Using Formulas to Evaluate Mathematical Expressions

Exercise Description

What is the advantage of solving equations on a spreadsheet? You can use formulas to make calculations, and help to solve a problem. You can also change the starting value, or seed value, and other values will automatically change if formulas were used to calculate them. If a variable in the formula changes, you can simply change the formula in one cell, Right Fill it, and the values will change accordingly.

Students will do this exercise when they have spent some time evaluating mathematical expressions using paper and pencil. Using a spreadsheet may be helpful to get them to understand why we use variables and to see how changing the seed value or the variable will change values.

Computer Activity

1. Students open the *Solving Math Expressions* template and begin with abstract problems using an input-output table.

	A	B	C	D	E	F	G	H	I	J	K	L	M	N	O
1	**Complete the input-output table using formulas.**														
2	y=x-3														
3	Input, x														
4	Output, y														
5															
6															
7	**Use input-output tables to solve these word problems:**														
8	**Tom is three years older than his sister, Audrey. Make an input-output table to show their ages.**														
9	Use formulas to insert Tom's age, then if you want to change the starting age, just change the seed value.														
10	Use formulas to calculate his sister's age. That way, if you want to extend the values for when														
11	Tom is older, just fill right.														
12	y=x-3 or A=T-3														
13	Tom	1	2	3	4	5									
14	Audrey														
15															
16	**Jake is 7 years old. He is now 3'1" tall. He grew 2 inches since last year.**														
17	If he grows at the same rate every year, how tall will he be when he is 14?														
18	Age														
19	Height in inches														
20	Extend the table to find out how tall he will be when he is 16 years old.														

Sheet1 / Sheet2 / Sheet3 /

Figure 36.1. The *Solving Math Expressions* template.

2. They then use the same formula to solve a word problem. They start by phrasing it as an equation. Tom is three years older than his sister Audrey is written as A=T–3. They generate values for Tom's age, T, beginning with a seed number, and then typing a formula to generate a range of values for T. In this way, they can change the starting point or seed value, and the spreadsheet will automatically generate numbers. We do not want negative ages for Audrey, so we change the seed from 1 to 3. Also, we can explore what will happen when the children get older by Right Filling the formulas.

	A	B	C	D	E	F
1	**Complete the input-outpu**					
2	y=x-3					
3	Input, x	1	=B3+1	=C3+1	=D3+1	=E3+1
4	Output, y	=B3-3	=C3-3	=D3-3	=E3-3	=F3-3

Figure 36.2. Students use formulas to generate values for x and y.

Formulas were used in the next example, to predict the height of Jake, who was 37" at age 7 and grew 2" per year.

7	8
37	=B18+2

The seed value was changed to predict the height of Steve, who was 48" at age 7 and grew 2" per year.

7	8
48	=B22+2

When the amount he grew each year changed after age 11, the formula was changed as follows:

10	11	12	13
=D27+2	=E27+2	=F27+3	=G27+3

3. In the next example, students enter the months of the year. They type in Jan and Feb, then highlight these two cells, and click on the fill handle in the bottom right corner of the cell, and drag right to fill names of the months. Initially, they go as far as October. They then enter in cell B35 the formula =B32+15 under February to calculate the value, then fill this formula right to calculate the amount Kyle will have saved each month. They copy the table and paste it, then modify it by changing the formula so that the target amount will be reached by October. They use trial and error to modify the formula in cell B35, then they Right Fill that formula.

32	Kyle wants to buy an MP3 player that costs $150.00. He already has $30.00 He saves $15.00 per month.												
33	It is January. When will he have enough money to buy it?												
34	**Month**	Jan	Feb	Mar	Apr	May	Jun	Jul	Aug	Sep	Oct	Nov	Dec	Jan
35	**$ amount**	30	45	60	75	90	105	120	135	150	165	180	195	210
36	Kyle goes to the store and finds that the MP3 player he wants costs $199. If he still saves $15.00												
37	per month, when will he have enough money to buy it?												
38	He does not want to wait longer than October.												
39	Copy the input-output table into the space below.												
40	Change the formula in the output row, so that Kyle will have enough money by September.												
41	Be sure to fill right each time you change the formula.												
42	**Month**	Jan	Feb	Mar	Apr	May	Jun	Jul	Aug	Sep	Oct		
43	**$ amount**	30	49	68	87	106	125	144	163	182	201		

Figure 36.3. Saving for an MP3 player.

Students finally solve the problem, using the formulas shown below:

Jan	Feb	Mar	Apr
30	=B39+19	=C39+19	=D39+19

4. In another example, students must choose the increment for x to solve the equation. They begin by giving x the value of 1, and increase by 1, but find they need smaller increments. They then increase by $0.50 to solve the problem for 3 or 5 people buying the gift. They need to change this increment if 2 or 10 people buy the gift. The formulas are inserted for them on the template (Figure 36.4), so that they can focus on one aspect of solving the problem.

x	3x	5x	2x	10x		x	2x	10x
	=A50*3	=A50*5	=A50*2	=A50*10			=G50*2	=10*G50
	=A51*3	=A51*5	=A51*2	=A51*10			=G51*2	=10*G51
	=A52*3	=A52*5	=A52*2	=A52*10			=G52*2	=10*G52

Figure 36.4. The increment formulas.

Using Formulas to Solve Mathematical Equations

Computer Activity

1. Students open the *Solving Math Equations* template and use the spreadsheet to generate a chart to solve the equation, 2x+7=4x+1. There are two equations that must be true, so students generate values to evaluate both equations, and they are true when the difference between the two solutions is zero. The equation is also true when the lines intersect on the chart.

2. Students click on the point where the lines intersect on the chart, and write the coordinates for when the expression is true.

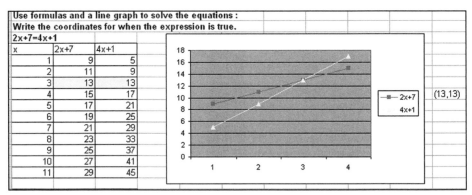

Figure 36.5. A completed problem on the *Solving Math Equations* template.

To find two numbers whose sum is 37 and whose difference is 13, students solve the equation x+y=37. If they solve for x-y=13, they would get negative numbers for the difference between numbers. They use ABS( ) to give the absolute value of the difference. See Figure 36.6, which shows the values and the formulas.

	A	B	C	D
37				
38	Number1	Number2	Total	Difference
39	10	=C39-A39	37	=ABS(A39-B39)
40	11	=C40-A40	37	=ABS(A40-B40)
41	12	=C41-A41	37	=ABS(A41-B41)
42	13	=C42-A42	37	=ABS(A42-B42)
43	14	=C43-A43	37	=ABS(A43-B43)
44	15	=C44-A44	37	=ABS(A44-B44)
45	16	=C45-A45	37	=ABS(A45-B45)
46	17	=C46-A46	37	=ABS(A46-B46)
47	18	=C47-A47	37	=ABS(A47-B47)
48	19	=C48-A48	37	=ABS(A48-B48)
49	20	=C49-A49	37	=ABS(A49-B49)
50	21	=C50-A50	37	=ABS(A50-B50)
51	22	=C51-A51	37	=ABS(A51-B51)
52	23	=C52-A52	37	=ABS(A52-B52)
53	24	=C53-A53	37	=ABS(A53-B53)
54	25	=C54-A54	37	=ABS(A54-B54)
55	26	=C55-A55	37	=ABS(A55-B55)

Figure 36.6. Solving differences with formulas.

3. Students use formulas to make a money calculator to help solve this problem: I have $3.45, and 3 more nickels than quarters. How many quarters do I have? They also enter a formula in the nickels column, as there are three more nickels than quarters. Students then make up their own money problem and use formulas to solve it.

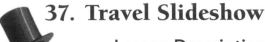

37. Travel Slideshow

Lesson Description

In this exercise, foreign language students learn about countries where the target language is spoken. They plan a trip to a foreign country and make a slideshow to share their findings with the class. Depending on their level of proficiency in the target language, they include some questions they would ask, or comment on something in a slide in the foreign language, or even narrate the whole slideshow in the target language. They investigate places to visit, places to stay, airfare to their destination, accommodations, food and transport, entertainment, and attractions. Students include spreadsheets in their slideshow: a currency converter and a budget for the trip. They also insert a spreadsheet with data that can be charted.

Higher-Order Thinking Skills	Spreadsheet Skills Practiced	Subject Areas and Standards Addressed
Apply knowledge of a language to read and understand online documents in the target language Synthesize and arrange information to create a slideshow to share information about their planned trip Understand the relationship between different currencies and create a currency converter Choose from options of places to visit and stay within a given budget	Insert a spreadsheet and chart into a slideshow Resize and move spreadsheets and charts Create and enter formulas	NETS•S: 1, 2, 3, 6 Foreign Language: 1.2; 1.3; 3.1; 3.2; 5.1 Mathematics: 2, 6

Computer Activity

1. Detailed directions are provided in the Student Instructions. In Part 1, students open a new PowerPoint document and make a slideshow about their planned trip to a foreign country. They use the Internet to find pictures to insert in the slideshow.

2. In Part 2, they open a new spreadsheet document and make a currency converter for their slideshow. Students convert from dollars to the currency in the target country and from that currency to dollars. They enter a formula on the spreadsheet to make the calculation. They may use the Universal Currency Converter at www.xe.com/ucc/ to get the current exchange rate.

3. In Part 3, students create a budget using the *Travel Budget* template. They use the Internet to find information about airfare, places to stay, and places of interest to visit at their destination. A completed budget for a trip to Paris appears in Figure 37.1.

Travel Budget for Trip to Paris				Je m'appelle Dominique
Expense	Francs	Dollars	Total $	Web address—source of info
Return airfare to Paris Northwest Airline (Chicago–Paris RT) (12/00–4/2001)		$464.00	$464.00	http://www.bestfares.com/travel_center/story.asp?id=10101928
Hotel le Stendahl (7 nights)		$83.00	$581.00	http://www.webscapades.com/france/paris/paris2.htm
Le Bistrot de Paris(Lunch) Magret de Canard du Gers a la bigarade de cerises noires, gaufre	176	$31.05	$31.05	menu—http://www.le-bistrot-de-paris.fr/carte_bdp_fr.htm
Brasserie Lipp (Dinner) Fricandeau de veau roti	275	$48.51	$48.51	menu—http://www.brasserie-lipp.fr/
Visit the Louvre museum	46	$8.11	$8.11	http://www.louvre.fr/
Elevator at Eiffel tower	42	$7.41	$7.41	http://www.smartweb.fr/visits/eiffel/index.html
5-day Visite Paris transport ticket	175	$30.87	$30.87	http://www.ratp.fr/Voy_q_eng/f_travel_pariv_eng.htm
2-day	90	$15.88	$15.88	http://www.ratp.fr/Voy_q_eng/f_travel_pariv_eng.htm
Visit Musee d'Orsay	40	$7.06	$7.06	http://www.musee-orsay.fr:8081/ORSAY/orsayNews/HTML.NSF/By+Filename/mosimple+modempl+acces+acces?OpenDocument
Total dollar amount			$1,193.88	
Other Useful Web Sites:				
Currency converter	http://www.xe.net/ucc/			
Paris Metro map	http://www.discoverfrance.com/gotoparis/visite3.html			
Additional money would be needed for:				
Food				
Shopping				
Additional sightseeing				

Figure 37.1. A completed travel budget.

4. In Part 4, students insert a chart into their slideshow that describes interesting details about the foreign country, such as the population of major cities.

Travel Slideshow
Student Instructions

My Plans to Visit a Foreign Country

Name: _____

PART 1: MAKE A SLIDESHOW

Open a new PowerPoint document and your Internet browser. Copy pictures from the Internet of the places you will visit and paste them into your PowerPoint slideshow. Acknowledge the source of the picture by pasting the Web address below the picture. Save your slideshow.

PART 2: INSERT A CURRENCY CONVERTER

1. Open your slideshow and insert a new slide.

2. Click on the Insert menu and select Object.

3. Click on Microsoft Excel Worksheet and type in your data. Format the font size to at least 36 points so that the data will be easy to read on the slide.

4. To get the current exchange rate, access an online currency converter, such as The Universal Currency Converter at www.xe.com/ucc/.

5. Insert the conversion formula. For instance, find out how many French francs you would get in exchange for one American dollar ($1.00). You then need to make a formula to convert dollars to francs. To do this, click in cell B2, type in = so that the computer knows this is a formula, click on the cell containing the dollar amount (A2), then type in * for multiply and the number of francs in a dollar from the Web site.

6. Insert two separate spreadsheets to make a currency converter from dollars to the foreign currency and from the foreign currency back to dollars.

	A	B
1	US$	French Francs
2	1	=A2*5.53644
3		

	A	B
1	French Francs	US $
2	1	=A2*180621
3		

Example. Currency converters.

continued

Travel Slideshow
Student Instructions continued

PART 3: INSERT A BUDGET

1. Use the Internet to plan how much money you will need for a week-long trip to the target country. Include traveling to and from your destination, transportation within the target country, hotel accommodations for a week, food, visits to attractions, and entertainment.

2. Open the *Travel Budget* template.

3. List your expenses in the first column.

4. Enter foreign currency amounts in column B, and convert these amounts to dollars in column C, using your currency converter. Use a formula to add the prices for column D, "Total $."

5. Copy and paste Web addresses in column E, "Web address—source of information." Click on the address in your Web browser, then right-click and select Copy. Open the spreadsheet, click in the appropriate cell in column E, right-click, and select Paste. The Web resources serve as references.

6. As you search for projected expenses for your trip, note any additional Web sites that provide good information for the traveler. Describe those and paste the addresses under "Other useful Web sites" on the template.

7. When you have completed your budget, insert it into your slideshow.

PART 4: INSERT A CHART

1. Click on the slide where you want to insert the chart, and insert a spreadsheet as described under Part 2.

2. Enter your data. For example, average temperature in major cities in summer, fall, winter, and spring; average yearly rainfall; or population in major cities (pie graph). Compare these to your hometown or city (bar graph). You may also compare the population in your target country with the country in which you live (bar graph).

3. Click inside the spreadsheet.

4. Click on the Insert menu and insert Chart, click on Finish.

5. To modify the chart, click on the Chart menu and select Chart Options.

6. You can move and resize a spreadsheet or a chart just like any graphic by clicking on it to reveal handlebars and dragging it to move. To resize, drag the handlebar diagonally.

continued

Travel Slideshow

Student Instructions continued

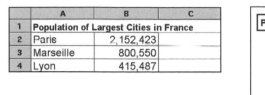

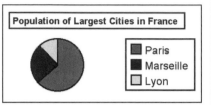

	A	B	C
1	Population of Largest Cities in France		
2	Paris	2,152,423	
3	Marseille	800,550	
4	Lyon	415,487	

Population of Largest Cities in France

■ Paris
■ Marseille
□ Lyon

Example. This table and pie chart show the populations of cities in France.

TECHNOLOGY CHECKLIST

Here is a technology checklist to help you follow all the steps for this lesson.

- Include slideshow title and name of author on first slide
- Include at least four other slides
- Change slide background
- Insert relevant clip art
- Insert relevant pictures from the Internet
- Acknowledge sources of pictures (Web addresses)
- Organize slides in logical order
- Insert an accurate currency converter
- Insert a budget
- Acknowledge sources of information for the budget (Web addresses)
- Insert a chart

In addition to completing these steps, you will be graded on the quality of content. Information must be accurate, clearly written in your own words, and relevant to planning a trip to the country. Write complete sentences, use proper punctuation, and check your spelling.

38. Analyzing Complex Patterns

Lesson Description

The lesson begins with a discussion about number patterns. Students give examples of patterns, counting by a number, going forward or backwards. The class examines how the differences between one number and the next in their patterns remains constant. Students open the *Complex Patterns* template (Figure 38.1) and look at the number patterns, working out the answers to the first few examples in their head. In the first two examples, they define the rule for the pattern by determining the difference between the numbers, and then they enter a formula to have the computer complete the pattern. They look at the other patterns, where the difference changes, first determining how the difference between numbers changes, and then calculating what the next number in the pattern will be. They insert formulas so that the computer will generate the pattern for them.

Higher-Order Thinking Skills	Spreadsheet Skills Practiced	Subject Areas and Standards Addressed
Analyze patterns and apply a rule Create original patterns	Change column width Enter an original formula Fill Right a formula Format spreadsheet to show or hide formulas	NETS•S: 3 Mathematics: 2

Figure 38.1. The *Complex Patterns* template.

#																
9	Pattern	96	80	64	48	32	16	0	-16	-32	-48	-64	-80	-96	-112	-128
10	Difference =16	16	16	16	16	16	16	16	16	16	16	16	16	16	16	
11	Difference remains constant															
12																
13	Pattern	1	5	12	22	35	51	70	92	117	145	176	210	247	287	330
14	First difference=3	4	7	10	13	16	19	22	25	28	31	34	37	40	43	
15	Difference changes by +3		+3	+3	+3	+3	+3	+3	+3	+3	+3	+3	+3	+3	+3	
16																
17	Pattern	1	2	4	7	11	16	22	29	37	46	56	67	79	92	106
18	First difference =+1	1	2	3	4	5	6	7	8	9	10	11	12	13	14	
19	Difference changes by +1		+1	+1	+1	+1	+1	+1	+1	+1	+1	+1	+1	+1	+1	

Figure 38.2. A sample of a completed Complex Patterns lesson.

#									
9	Pattern	96	80	64	48	=E9-E10	=F9-F10	=G9-G10	=H9-H10
10	Difference =16	16	16	16	16	16	16	16	16
11	Difference remains constant								
12									
13	Pattern	1	5	12	22	=E13+E14	=F13+F14	=G13+G14	=H13+H14
14	First difference=3	4	7	10	13	=E14+3	=F14+3	=G14+3	=H14+3
15	Difference changes by +3		+3	+3	+3	+3	+3	+3	+3
16									
17	Pattern	1	2	4	7	11	=F17+F18	=G17+G18	=H17+H18
18	First difference =+1	1	2	3	4	=E18+1	=F18+1	=G18+1	=H18+1
19	Difference changes by +1		+1	+1	+1	+1	+1	+1	+1

Figure 38.3. The same lesson as in Figure 38.2, with the formulas showing.

Computer Activity

1. Open the *Complex Patterns* template. Text color has been formatted to help identify the difference between numbers (red), and how much that difference changes (blue). The blue font cells have been formatted as text, so that you can enter +3 and it shows as +3. (If it is formatted as a number, then Excel makes the calculation and +3 shows as 3.) If a number is too large for a cell, the number will show up as ###, and you will need to widen the columns.

2. Automatically resize the columns by double-clicking on the line between the column headers.

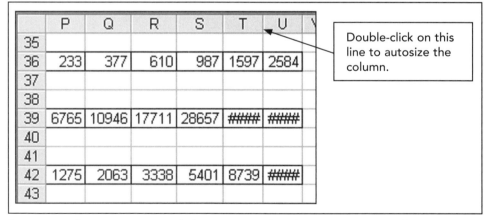

Figure 38.4. If #### appears instead of an entry in a cell, widen the cell automatically.

3. Enter a formula by clicking in the cell where you want the formula to go and press the = key. Use the mouse to select the cell you want as the first variable in the formula, press + or – and the amount, and press Enter.

4. Right Fill a formula by clicking on the fill handle (the small black square on the bottom right corner of the cell containing the formula) so that the mouse changes to a cross. Drag over the cells where you want the formula to go.

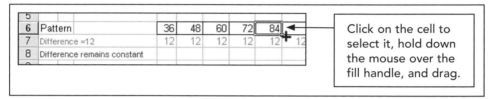

Figure 38.5. Adding formulas to a series of cells can be done with dragging.

5. The default setting in Excel only shows formulas in the insertion bar. Show formulas in the spreadsheet cells by clicking on the Tools menu, then select Options. Click on the View tab and place a check mark next to Formulas.

39. Probability with Coins and Dice

Lesson Description

Using a template that automatically generates tossing coins and throwing dice can help students see how a larger sample provides a more predictable result. Students start by tossing coins on their own, in small groups.

Higher-Order Thinking Skills	Spreadsheet Skills Practiced	Subject Areas and Standards Addressed
Devise a way to test a hypothesis by creating an experiment	Insert a chart	NETS•S: 3, 6
	Label a chart series and format the Y-axis	Mathematics: 5
Analyze the results of the experiment, and its implications for the chances of getting heads or tails when a coin is tossed, or a specific number when dice are rolled	Use the AutoSum function	
	Insert a formula to calculate percentage	
Predict the outcome of dice throws and coin tosses	Generate random numbers and use the IF function (Extension)	
Understand the meaning of probability		
Create a formula to make calculations		
Analyze how the computer generates random numbers (Extension)		

Computer Activity

1. Students open the *Probability* template, enter their names, and print it out. Each printed copy will have numbers on it that are randomly generated by the computer, simulating coin tosses and dice throws. The template also has blank tables for students to enter their own results as they toss coins and throw dice, noting either heads or tails. (Make sure to have the students use the hard copy to enter their results rather than the computer, as the computer generates new random numbers every time a change is made to the spreadsheet.)

2. Each student tosses a coin 10 times and records the results (heads or tails) on the hard copy. Students tally their scores, then form groups of two or three to gather group data.

3. Besides student totals, they tally the number of heads and tails generated by the computer from each student's print-out, and write the totals in the Coin Toss table on the template's right side (Figure 39.1).

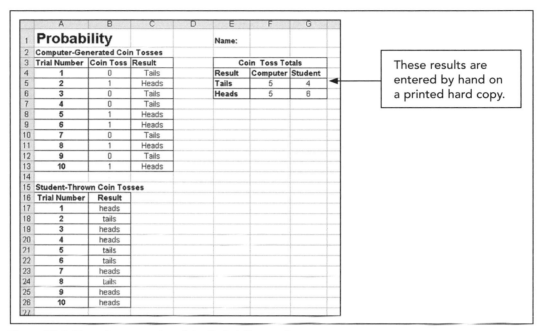

	A	B	C	D	E	F	G
1	**Probability**				Name:		
2	Computer-Generated Coin Tosses						
3	Trial Number	Coin Toss	Result		Coin Toss Totals		
4	1	0	Tails		Result	Computer	Student
5	2	1	Heads		Tails	5	4
6	3	0	Tails		Heads	5	6
7	4	0	Tails				
8	5	1	Heads				
9	6	1	Heads				
10	7	0	Tails				
11	8	1	Heads				
12	9	0	Tails				
13	10	1	Heads				
14							
15	Student-Thrown Coin Tosses						
16	Trial Number	Result					
17	1	heads					
18	2	tails					
19	3	heads					
20	4	heads					
21	5	tails					
22	6	tails					
23	7	heads					
24	8	tails					
25	9	heads					
26	10	heads					
27							

These results are entered by hand on a printed hard copy.

Figure 39.1. The coin toss section of the *Probability* template.

4. Students collect data in the same way for throwing dice. They throw the dice 20 times and record the results. The computer generates random numbers between 1 and 6 in cells B 31–50. Students total the scores on the printed copy, and enter them in the Dice-Throwing table on the right side (Figure 39.2).

It isn't necessary to know how the coin tossing and dice-throwing formulas work to complete this lesson, but if this interests you, see the Extension for this lesson.

5. Each student group opens the *Probability Totals* template. The groups share their results with each other, so that each group can enter the class data on the spreadsheet. (A sample completed template is available on the CD-ROM.)

6. Students use the AutoSum button on the Standard toolbar to calculate the coin toss totals. To calculate the percentage, they take the total number of tails (B19) or heads (C19) and divide it by the total number of coin tosses (B19+C19). The formula =B19/(B19+C19) calculates the percentage of tails. They complete the Coin Toss Summary table on the right.

AutoSum Icon

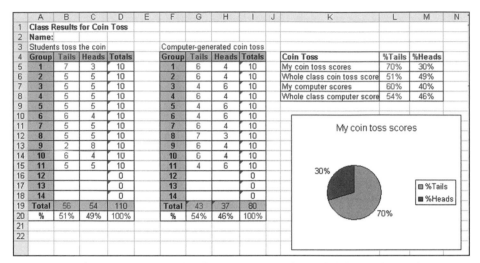

Figure 39.2. After gathering class data for coin tosses on the *Probability Totals* template, students make pie charts showing the results.

7. Using the coin toss data, students make two pie charts, one showing their own group's coin toss scores and one showing the coin toss scores of the whole class. Remember, to make a chart, highlight the area you want to chart, click on the Insert menu, then on Chart. Choose a pie chart and click Finish. To show the percentages on the pie chart, right-click the chart, click on Chart Options, click on the Data Labels tab, and click on Show Percent.

8. Students compare the two pie charts. They should notice that the percentage gets closer to 50% when the group is larger.

9. Further down on the same template, students enter group totals for throwing the dice.

10. Students sum the totals for the coin tosses and calculate percentages. To calculate the percentage, they take the total number of times the dice landed on a number and divide it by the total number of dice throws, for example 44/220. They then enter the data in the table to compare data from dice thrown by students and computer-generated dice throws, and complete the Dice-Throwing Summary table on the right.

11. Have the class discuss why, if the sample was large enough, each of the six numbers should be thrown 16.67%, or one sixth, of the time.

12. Using the dice-throwing data, students make two bar charts, one showing their own group's dice-throwing scores, and one showing the scores of the whole class. Remember, to make a bar chart, highlight the data that should appear in the chart. Click on the Insert menu and on Chart, click on Column under Chart Type, and select Finish. To change the numbers on the Y-axis to percentages, double-click on the Value Axis (Y-axis), click on the Number tab, click on Percentage under Category, and choose 0 decimal places.

13. Have students add a green line to the chart at the 16.67% point. On the second chart, they see that group scores, or scores for a larger number of trials, fall closer to the probability estimate of 16.67% than individual results, or scores for fewer trials.

Extensions

- Students calculate percentages using scrap paper or insert formulas on the spreadsheet to make the calculation for them. To use a formula, start by entering = so that the computer knows that a formula is being entered. Then click on the total in cell B19 and divide it number by the total number of coin tosses in cell D19. The formula would look like this: =B19/D19. Students could then Fill Right this by clicking on the cell containing the formula, dragging the mouse over the cells they want to generalize the formula to, clicking on the Edit menu, clicking on Fill, and then on Right. The same procedure may be done to calculate formulas for dice-throwing (Figure 39.3).

Student dice		
Group	One	Two
1	2	5
2	4	4
3	3	0
4	1	0
5	5	2
6	3	2
7	5	2
8	3	3
9	4	3
10	4	5
11	3	4
12		
13		
14		
Total	=SUM(B45:B5	=SUM(C45:C55)
%	=B59/H59	=C59/H59

Figure 39.3.
Sample rows showing formulas.

- Advanced students may want to understand how the computer generated random coin tosses and random dice throws.

  To get random tosses of the coin, random numbers are generated in column B, then converted to heads and tails in column C.

  =RAND() returns a random number between 1 and 0. These values are entered in column B

=IF(B4<=0.5,"Tails","Heads") returns tails for numbers less than or equal to 0.5, and heads for numbers greater than 0.5. This formula is entered in column C, converting the random number into tails or heads.

To get random throws of the dice, between 1 and 6, this formula is used: =ROUNDUP(RAND()*6,0)

=RAND() returns a random number between 1 and 0.

*6 multiplies this random number by six, but if formatted to 0 decimal places, it will give values between 0 and 6. We do not want zeros.

ROUNDUP (Cell address zero,0) rounds a number in a designated cell up, away from 0, and 0 makes it an integer as it indicates the number of digits to which you want to round.

40. Comparing Countries

Lesson Description

Students pick two countries from four of the following continents: North America, South America, Asia, Europe, and Africa. They use print or online resources to find factual information, which they enter in the *Comparing Countries* template. They enter formulas to calculate the population density and the total GDP (Gross Domestic Product). They then sort the information by largest area, largest population, largest per capita GDP, and highest Human Development Index (HDI, a United Nations measurement). They write two sentences each time they sort the data to interpret the results. The class discusses their findings, shares their data, and compares countries in terms of size, population, GDP, and HDI. The class discusses the effect each of these measures might have on the quality of life for a country's inhabitants.

Higher-Order Thinking Skills	Spreadsheet Skills Practiced	Subject Areas and Standards Addressed
Compare statistics for countries, sort from the largest to the smallest, richest to the poorest, highest to lowest HDI. Interpret the meaning of statistics about countries	Use a Web browser to find information Copy data from a Web page and paste it into a spreadsheet Sort data according to a selected column Insert columns Insert a formula and generalize that formula	NETS•S: 4, 5 Mathematics: 2 Social Studies: III, VI, VII

Computer Activity

1. Students open the *Comparing Countries* template, and enter data for two countries on each of the four continents they picked (eight countries in all).

2. Students click on the heading of Column E, then click on the Insert menu and on Column. Enter a formula to calculate the population density by dividing the area by the population. For example, in Figure 40.1, =D2/C2 was entered to calculate the population density of Canada.

3. To fill the formula down, students click on the cell containing the formula, click on the corner of the cell, and drag the fill handle down.

4. They click on the heading of Column F, then click on the Insert menu and on Column. Students enter a formula to calculate the total GDP by multiplying the population by the per capita GDP. For example, in Figure 40.1, =D2*F2 was entered to calculate the total GDP of Canada. Students fill this formula down in the same way as the population density formula.

5. To make comparisons, have students sort the data. Have them highlight cells from Cell A2 to H9, click on the Data menu, choose Sort, then click on the arrow under Sort By to select a criterion for sorting (for example, Area).

6. After students have sorted according to a criterion, have them write two sentences on their findings in the space beneath the table.

7. Have students continue to sort the data based on various criteria. Have them write additional sentences to report their findings.

	A	B	C	D	E	F	G	H
1	**Comparing Countries**							
2	Country	Capital	Area (sq. mile)	Population	Density of Population	Per Capita GDP	Total GDP	Human Development Index
3	Canada	Ottawa	3,849,670	31,900,000	8	$29,800	$950,620,000,000	0.943
4	USA	Washington, D.C.	3,717,796	293,600,000	79	$37,800	$11,098,080,000,000	0.939
5	Madagascar	Antananarivo	226,656	17,500,000	77	$800	$14,000,000,000	0.469
6	Botswana	Gaborone	224,606	1,700,000	8	$9,000	$15,300,000,000	0.589
7	Brazil	Brasilia	3,300,154	179,100,000	54	$7,600	$1,361,160,000,000	0.775
8	Paraguay	Asuncion	157,046	6,000,000	38	$4,700	$28,200,000,000	0.751
9	Bulgaria	Sofia	42,822	7,800,000	182	$7,600	$59,280,000,000	0.942
10	Liechtenstein	Vaduz	62	30,000	484	$25,000	$750,000,000	N/A
11								
12	Sort by area and interpret your findings:							
13	Liechtenstein is by far the tiniest country of the eight.							
14	Several Botswanas could fit inside one Canada.							
15	Sort by population and interpret your findings:							
16	Liechtenstein's population is smaller than that of New Berlin.							
17	The third largest country, Canada, is far behind the second largest, Brazil.							
18	Sort by per capita GDP and interpret your findings:							
19	Madagascar has one of the lowest GDPs in the world.							
20	The USA has one of the highest in the world.							
21	Sort by HDI and interpret your findings:							
22	Canada has a higher development index than the USA.							
23	Madagascar, which also has the lowest GDP, has the lowest HDI.							

Figure 40.1. A completed Comparing Countries lesson.

Extension

After sharing information in the class, students can compare population density, per capita GDP, or the Human Development Index between continents. Have them share all the data they have collected about countries by copying and pasting their information on the *Comparing Countries–Class* template. They can then sort the data and interpret their findings.

Appendix

ISTE National Educational Technology Standards (NETS) and Performance Indicators for Students

The National Educational Technology Standards for students are divided into six broad categories. Standards within each category are to be introduced, reinforced, and mastered by students. These categories provide a framework for linking performance indicators, listed by grade level, to the standards. Teachers can use these standards and performance indicators as guidelines for planning technology-based activities in which students achieve success in learning, communication, and life skills.

1. **Basic operations and concepts**

   - Students demonstrate a sound understanding of the nature and operation of technology systems.

   - Students are proficient in the use of technology.

2. **Social, ethical, and human issues**

   - Students understand the ethical, cultural, and societal issues related to technology.

   - Students practice responsible use of technology systems, information, and software.

   - Students develop positive attitudes toward technology uses that support lifelong learning, collaboration, personal pursuits, and productivity.

3. **Technology productivity tools**

   - Students use technology tools to enhance learning, increase productivity, and promote creativity.

   - Students use productivity tools to collaborate in constructing technology-enhanced models, preparing publications, and producing other creative works.

4. **Technology communications tools**

   - Students use telecommunications to collaborate, publish, and interact with peers, experts, and other audiences.

   - Students use a variety of media and formats to communicate information and ideas effectively to multiple audiences.

5. **Technology research tools**

   - Students use technology to locate, evaluate, and collect information from a variety of sources.

   - Students use technology tools to process data and report results.

- Students evaluate and select new information resources and technological innovations based on the appropriateness to specific tasks.

6. **Technology problem-solving and decision-making tools**

   - Students use technology resources for solving problems and making informed decisions.

   - Students employ technology in the development of strategies for solving problems in the real world.

Profiles for Technology-Literate Students

All students should have opportunities to demonstrate the following performances. Numbers in parentheses following each performance indicator refer to the standards category to which the performance is linked.

Grades PreK–2

Prior to completion of Grade 2, students will:

1. Use input devices (e.g., mouse, keyboard, remote control) and output devices (e.g., monitor, printer) to successfully operate computers, VCRs, audiotapes, and other technologies. (1)

2. Use a variety of media and technology resources for directed and independent learning activities. (1, 3)

3. Communicate about technology using developmentally appropriate and accurate terminology. (1)

4. Use developmentally appropriate multimedia resources (e.g., interactive books, educational software, elementary multimedia encyclopedias) to support learning. (1)

5. Work cooperatively and collaboratively with peers, family members, and others when using technology in the classroom. (2)

6. Demonstrate positive social and ethical behaviors when using technology. (2)

7. Practice responsible use of technology systems and software. (2)

8. Create developmentally appropriate multimedia products with support from teachers, family members, or student partners. (3)

9. Use technology resources (e.g., puzzles, logical thinking programs, writing tools, digital cameras, drawing tools) for problem solving, communication, and illustration of thoughts, ideas, and stories. (3, 4, 5, 6)

10. Gather information and communicate with others using telecommunications, with support from teachers, family members, or student partners. (4)

Grades 3–5

Prior to completion of Grade 5 students will:

1. Use keyboards and other common input and output devices (including adaptive devices when necessary) efficiently and effectively. (1)

2. Discuss common uses of technology in daily life and the advantages and disadvantages those uses provide. (1, 2)

3. Discuss basic issues related to responsible use of technology and information and describe personal consequences of inappropriate use. (2)

4. Use general purpose productivity tools and peripherals to support personal productivity, remediate skill deficits, and facilitate learning throughout the curriculum. (3)

5. Use technology tools (e.g., multimedia authoring, presentation, Web tools, digital cameras, scanners) for individual and collaborative writing, communication, and publishing activities to create knowledge products for audiences inside and outside the classroom. (3, 4)

6. Use telecommunications efficiently and effectively to access remote information, communicate with others in support of direct and independent learning, and pursue personal interests. (4)

7. Use telecommunications and online resources (e.g., e-mail, online discussions, Web environments) to participate in collaborative problem-solving activities for the purpose of developing solutions or products for audiences inside and outside the classroom. (4, 5)

8. Use technology resources (e.g., calculators, data collection probes, videos, educational software) for problem-solving, self-directed learning, and extended learning activities. (5, 6)

9. Determine when technology is useful and select the appropriate tool(s) and technology resources to address a variety of tasks and problems. (5, 6)

10. Evaluate the accuracy, relevance, appropriateness, comprehensiveness, and bias of electronic information sources. (6)

Grades 6–8

Prior to completion of Grade 8 students will:

1. Apply strategies for identifying and solving routine hardware and software problems that occur during everyday use. (1)

2. Demonstrate knowledge of current changes in information technologies and the effect those changes have on the workplace and society. (2)

3. Exhibit legal and ethical behaviors when using information and technology, and discuss consequences of misuse. (2)

4. Use content-specific tools, software, and simulations (e.g., environmental probes, graphing calculators, exploratory environments, Web tools) to support learning and research. (3, 5)

5. Apply productivity/multimedia tools and peripherals to support personal productivity, group collaboration, and learning throughout the curriculum. (3, 6)

6. Design, develop, publish, and present products (e.g., Web pages, videotapes) using technology resources that demonstrate and communicate curriculum concepts to audiences inside and outside the classroom. (4, 5, 6)

7. Collaborate with peers, experts, and others using telecommunications and collaborative tools to investigate curriculum-related problems, issues, and information, and to develop solutions or products for audiences inside and outside the classroom. (4, 5)

8. Select and use appropriate tools and technology resources to accomplish a variety of tasks and solve problems. (5, 6)

9. Demonstrate an understanding of concepts underlying hardware, software, and connectivity, and of practical applications to learning and problem solving. (1, 6)

10. Research and evaluate the accuracy, relevance, appropriateness, comprehensiveness, and bias of electronic information sources concerning real-world problems. (2, 5, 6)

Grades 9–12

Prior to completion of Grade 12 students will:

1. Identify capabilities and limitations of contemporary and emerging technology resources and assess the potential of these systems and services to address personal, lifelong learning, and workplace needs. (2)

2. Make informed choices among technology systems, resources, and services. (1,2)

3. Analyze advantages and disadvantages of widespread use of and reliance on technology in the workplace and in society as a whole. (2)

4. Demonstrate and advocate for legal and ethical behavior among peers, family, and community regarding the use of technology and information. (2)

5. Use technology tools and resources for managing and communicating personal/professional information (e.g., finances, schedules, addresses, purchases, correspondence). (3, 4)

6. Evaluate technology-based options, including distance and distributed education, for lifelong learning. (5)

7. Routinely and efficiently use online information resources to meet needs for collaboration, research, publications, communications, and productivity. (4, 5, 6)

8. Select and apply technology tools for research, information analysis, problem solving, and decision making in content learning. (4, 5)

9. Investigate and apply expert systems, intelligent agents, and simulations in real-world situations. (3, 5, 6)

10. Collaborate with peers, experts, and others to contribute a content-related knowledge base by using technology to compile, synthesize, produce, and disseminate information, models, and other creative works. (4, 5, 6)